12/6

FERNAND PORTAL
1855–1926

FERNAND PORTAL

FERNAND PORTAL
(1855–1926)
APOSTLE OF UNITY

✳

From the French *Monsieur Portal*
by H. Hemmer

✳

TRANSLATED AND
EDITED BY

ARTHUR T. MACMILLAN

LONDON
MACMILLAN & CO LTD
NEW YORK · ST MARTIN'S PRESS
1961

MACMILLAN AND COMPANY LIMITED
London Bombay Calcutta Madras Melbourne

THE MACMILLAN COMPANY OF CANADA LIMITED
Toronto

ST MARTIN'S PRESS INC
New York

PRINTED IN GREAT BRITAIN

INTRODUCTION

THE present interest in the possibility of the reunion of, or at any rate of more friendly relations between the Churches, heightened as it has been by His Holiness Pope John XXIII's summoning of a General Council, seemed to make it opportune to put before the English reading public a portrait of the remarkable man who is the subject of this short book.

It is the story of a French Lazarist priest who chanced, when fairly young, to meet Charles Lindley, 2nd Viscount Halifax, the well-known leader of the English Church Union, from which chance meeting there developed a lifelong friendship between them, and a lifelong collaboration in attempts to bring about a corporate reunion of the Anglican Church and the Church of Rome — an attempt which culminated in the well-known 'Conversations' at Malines, under the presidency of Cardinal Mercier, in the early 1920s. The story of the Abbé Portal's infinite patience, unbounded charity, and unshakeable faith in the midst of many disappointments, cannot but serve as an example and inspiration to all working for the same object.

The French book of which this is a translation, was published in Paris in 1947, under the title *H. Hemmer, Monsieur Portal, prêtre de la Mission (1855–1926)*. It is a composite book, which was edited and arranged by Canon Hemmer, who unfortunately died before publication. Canon Hemmer was a great friend of Portal and one of the Catholic theologians at the Malines Conversations, and himself wrote four of the chapters : the others being written by friends more closely acquainted with different aspects of Portal's life and work.

I have shortened the original very considerably, omitting altogether three chapters — Nos. 8, 9, and 13 — which cannot, I think, be of any contemporary interest, and for the same reason have pruned some of the others. I have also rearranged the order, putting the chapter on the Appartement in the rue de Grenelle after the one on the Foundation of the Seminary of St. Vincent of Paul, which chronologically is its proper place. The last chapter, which

Introduction

I have renamed 'The Apostle of Love' is very much
shortened; but it gives, I hope, a living picture of that
side of M. Portal's character which was little known to
those who met him only in his great work for unity, and
seems a fitting epilogue to the story of this great Christian.
But, apart from some rather copious footnotes to some of
the chapters, which where mine are identified by my initials
'A. T. M.', and a few places where I have printed a document in full, *e.g.* the Appendix containing Archbishop's
Benson's letter to Lord Halifax dated 15 October 1894
(p. 177) and Cardinal Mercier's letter to the Archbishop
of Canterbury (Dr. Davidson) dated 25 October 1925
(p. 158), there is nothing in this translation which does not
appear in the original. As this is a composite work, I will
give the names of the authors of the various chapters :
Chapters 1 to 3 inclusive, and Chapter 9 are by Canon
Hemmer. Chapters 5 to 8 inclusive are by the Abbé
Gratieux ; also about the first half of Chapter 4, the second
half of which was written by the Abbé Giaume — the text
shows where the break comes. Finally Chapter 10 is from
the pen of the Reverend Father M.-A. Dieux.

My thanks are especially due to the following: the
Reverend H. R. T. Brandreth, O.G.S. of St. Georges, Paris,
and the Reverend J. C. Dickinson, of Pembroke College,
Cambridge, for much helpful advice and hospitality; the
present Earl of Halifax for permission to copy and use the
five letters appearing at pp. 134-138, and also to Major
Ingram, archivist to the late Earl, for the trouble he has taken
to find them; the Reverend F. P. Coleman, Secretary of the
Church Union for his help in finding the English originals
of some of Lord Halifax's speeches which appear in Chapter
2; and last (though not least) the proprietors and staff of the
Church Times for similar help in looking up old files of their
newspaper.

Finally I would like to record the great privilege I feel
at having been entrusted with the task of translating into
English the life of so great a Christian as Fernand Portal.
I hope that readers will judge the result worthy of its subject.

A. T. M.

CONTENTS

PART ONE
THE ANGLO-ROMAN CAMPAIGN

CHAPTER I

Prelude

FERNAND-ÉTIENNE PORTAL, the son of Pierre Portal and his wife Louise Lafabrier, was born on 14 August 1855, at Laroque, which is a village in the department of Hérault, near the Cévennes mountains. He was baptized in the village church on 16 August. The question asked about the infant John Baptist, 'What manner of child shall this be?' must occur to most Christian parents of any new-born child, particularly a son. But no sign seemed to foretell what the future held for this one, and it was not until he was nearly 3 years old that an incident occurred which seemed to show that Providence had particular designs, of which M. Portal gives a very matter-of-fact account.

When I was nearly three years old, illness had brought me to death's door. One evening the doctor thought that I would not last the night, and warned my mother of this, telling her that he would not be calling again to see me. When my father returned, he found my mother and grandmother in tears by the side of the small patient whose death they were expecting at any moment. At first he felt great indignation that the unfeeling doctor had dared to speak so to my mother; however, on second thoughts he went out without saying where he was going. In our Cévennes mountains there is an ancient sanctuary to which, for centuries, catholic pilgrimages have been made. The neighbouring parishes attend each year. In old days the faithful would often march there in procession, reciting prayers or chanting psalms.

It is a good three hours' walk from Laroque to the small ruined church of Notre-Dame du Suc, since rebuilt, which is consecrated to the Blessed Virgin Mary.

It was there [continues M. Portal] that my father prayed for

3

a miracle to happen. He got to the chapel about midnight, and without disturbing the hermit in charge of it, he prayed for a long time outside the door. He promised the blessed Virgin that if she obtained my restoration to health, I should be consecrated to her : that for three years I would wear her colours : that on three successive anniversaries I would be brought to the chapel, and that, if later I expressed a wish to embrace the religious life, he would offer no opposition. He then came home, and it was two o'clock in the morning before he returned. To relieve the anxiety caused by his long absence he told those round my cot what he had done. There had been no change in my condition, and the night ended sadly for the family which had already suffered the loss of a small elder child. The next day, however, there was a slight improvement, and a few days later I was definitely on the road to recovery.

Fernand Portal's parents never seemed to have any definite plan to give their son to the Church ; nevertheless when the time came for him to begin his lessons, they entrusted him to a relation who was a parish priest in the diocese of Nîmes. This priest's influence was probably responsible, in part at any rate, for the boy's later wish to take Holy Orders. In 1867 the Abbé Portal was obliged, owing to a change of residence, to return Fernand to his parents : the boy, however, was very keen to continue his studies, and in 1868 he went to a small boarding school at Beaucaire. A year later he was sent to another school at Montpellier, where he stayed from 1869 to 1874, and completed his secondary education.

Fernand Portal was greatly attracted towards a military career, and, for a time, this seriously rivalled the claims of a religious vocation. It was only after much hesitation that he chose the priesthood. At that time it was his ambition to do missionary work among the heathen and to become a Lazarist with that in view. His parents had been urging him to make up his mind, and his letter informing them of his decision is remarkable both for its firm tone and its loving deference.

4

Prelude

MY DARLING PARENTS,

The uncertainty you have been in is at last coming to an end, and I will end it forthwith by saying that I now hope one day to become a good priest. For the last five years two careers have been in my mind: the army and the priesthood. After much mental struggle and helped by divine grace and by wise advisers, I have at last made my choice. As I have already told you, I firmly believe that I have a vocation for the sacred ministry. My dear parents, I do indeed mean to be a priest, but not a parish priest. My tastes and my character alike draw me towards life in a religious community, and my one wish now is to become a good Lazarist, a child of St. Vincent of Paul. You are, I am sure, already envisaging the cruel separation which this will entail: but remember that you gave me to the blessed Virgin when I was three years old. Ah, if my father, when praying in the church of Our Lady of Suc while I lay dying in my cot, had been asked to choose between his child dying and becoming a missionary, he would not have hesitated. You gave me to Mary: consummate the gift; through such a good mother we will be granted the courage of which we stand in such need. I shall await your answer, which I hope will be by return of post, with great anxiety. Please listen only to the promptings of your deepest religious feelings, and I feel sure that, though you may shed many tears, you will answer 'Go where God calls you'. I end this letter with my deepest love. Fernand the missionary will still be your loving and respectful son. His love will, if possible, be even greater for his brave parents, of whom he is proud to call himself the most grateful and obedient son

PORTAL

There was no lengthy opposition to his plans. His father did advance certain objections, as it involved a big sacrifice for him. He was, however, a man of his word, and he had made a promise to the blessed Virgin. His reply, though definite, ends sadly, 'The blessed Virgin claims you back; for this reason only I am letting you go'.

Fernand Portal was received into the congregation of the

Mission ¹ on 14 August, his nineteenth birthday. Two years later, on 15 August 1876, he took the vows.

Neither letters nor diaries give us any detailed account of this young Lazarist's noviciate or theological studies. The ordinary curriculum then in vogue at St-Lazare prescribed, during the second year of the noviciate, a course in philosophy additional to the philosophy which the noviciate was supposed to have read before being admitted. Three years were devoted to theological studies. The text-books then in use in French seminaries were elementary manuals of theology (Bouvier, Vincent, Bonal, Schouppe, etc.). But at St-Lazare, as at St-Sulpice, oral teaching from experts in the vocational life provided a useful addition to the learning acquired from books. Catholic Institutes had but recently been founded (in 1876) and had not yet resulted in that striking intellectual and theological revival among the clergy of France which was such a striking feature of the last part of the century and in which M. Portal collaborated with intelligence and sympathy. Throughout his life M. Portal never doubted that he had been divinely inspired in his first inclination towards the congregation of the Mission. From the first he was in his element among the children of St. Vincent of Paul, and until his death he believed that divine Providence had called him to be a priest of the Mission. His own affectionate nature was seen at its best in the atmosphere of unaffected piety, of good fellowship, and of love which informed the relationship between him and his colleagues. The development of the spiritual and mystical life of the young men at St-Lazare owed much to the traditions handed down from St. Vincent of Paul. The complete works of the saintly founder had not then been published, and vulgarized as they were in Mr. Coste's large edition. But the essential parts of both the letters and the 'Entretiens' existed, and formed a

¹ This is the name of the congregation of secular priests living under religious vows, founded by St. Vincent de Paul in 1625. They are popularly known as 'Lazarists', from the priory of St-Lazare, which was St. Vincent's headquarters in Paris.—A. T. M.

precious basis on which was developed the general intellectual outlook and the spiritual life of the community.
Their influence on M. Portal was profound, and he later
recognized in the effects of that influence the debt he owed
to his elders — his spiritual fathers.

The five years' training (1876 to 1880) in a cloistered
seminary were interspersed with a succession of ordinations :
the tonsure and minor orders in 1878, the subdiaconate in
December of the same year; the diaconate on 7 June 1879,
and finally the priesthood on 22 May 1880. The even tenor
of Fernand Portal's life among his co-students was interrupted
by a breakdown in health, as a result of which he was, in
1878, sent to teach in the secondary school at Tours. This
warning as regards his health was remembered by his
superiors when the time came to choose his life's work. 'My
health was far from good during my period at the mother
house of the Lazarists' was the entry in M. Portal's private
diary. Throughout his life he was to remain liable to these
serious breakdowns, which far from being a matter of com-
plaint he regarded as a providential help to his life's work.
He writes :

> I often quote the saying of St. Teresa that thanks to God she
> has always had ill health, not only for its inherent truth, but also
> because, if I dare apply it to myself, I can never sufficiently thank
> God for having sent ill health to me. Success and failure, good
> and ill health, can all help us along the path which God wills for
> us, and often frustrations and sickness do so most surely. It was
> so with me.

The wheels of God grind slowly, however, and it was a
disappointment to young Portal to see fading the hopes of
becoming a foreign missionary which had so attracted him
in youth and probably inspired his vocation. No sooner
was he ordained than he asked his Superior General to be
sent to China; a request which was tactfully put on one
side, and instead he was appointed professor of philosophy
at a large seminary at Oran. He failed, however, to

complete an academic year, being struck down with an attack of blood spitting. He writes in his diary:

In the first month I had four attacks in one day. I made my confession, offering my life to God. This was more by way of Christian prudence than belief that I was dying, as I never for a moment gave up hope of recovery.

He did indeed recover, but remained subject to such attacks for upwards of twenty years. It was this very weakness which led to that meeting between M. Portal and Lord Halifax (described in the next chapter) which settled definitely for him the purpose and direction of his life's work.

But meanwhile he was for several years moved about from pillar to post. He was sent from Oran to Lisbon, then to the large seminary at Nice, and finally (in 1882) to that at Cahors, where for four years he taught dogmatic theology. In 1886, following a renewed attack of blood spitting, he had to give up, and in 1887 went to the milder climate of Lisbon, having in the interval undertaken certain missions in Spain. During these trying years Portal developed both spiritually and intellectually. He learnt both Spanish and Portuguese, and himself a keen student of men, observed carefully the customs and institutions of these countries. A carefully chosen course of reading broadened his outlook, while the abiding threat of illness served as a constant reminder of the transitoriness of life.

A well-known writer, Mr. Eugene Tavernier, who met M. Portal a little later (about 1894) and subsequently came to know him intimately, has left this striking portrait.

M. Portal was then aged about thirty-nine years, but looked younger. He was well set up, with black hair over a high distinguished forehead: his features were well modelled with the firm mouth and chin which indicate a forceful character. The whole was lighted up by a pair of eyes in which shone both intelligence and spirituality, and there emanated a liveliness which seemed a combination of cordiality, modesty, and refinement. Such is my earliest memory, maintained by a most intimate relationship extending over thirty years. M. Portal inspired confidence, which he was always ready to reciprocate. In this faithful and zealous Lazarist priest was exemplified the most perfect form of friendship — not only affectionate, but full of loving care for its object. Simplicity was the outstanding characteristic of the Abbé Portal's nature. In every branch of the ministry — propaganda, retreats, teaching, administration, writing, and the works of corporal charity, he set himself to achieve that simplicity which St. Vincent had taught by precept and example.

Such a nature needed only the opportunity to develop such a friendship as would serve a great cause.

CHAPTER 2

From Friendship to Apostolate—Lord Halifax

THE first meeting between M. Portal and Lord Halifax, which took place in the island of Madeira at the end of 1889, was the starting-point of his life's work as apostle for Christian union, particularly union with the Church of England. The extremely intimate friendship which developed between him and this High Church English aristocrat greatly influenced M. Portal's views on the methods to be used in trying to overcome the differences and bring nearer to each other the two Churches which had been separated for so many centuries.

M. Portal landed in Madeira in October 1889. He was then 34 years old, and can have had as little idea of what would become his life's work as had St. Vincent of Paul, at about the same age, that his would be the evangelization of the poor and the reformation of the French clergy.

There then existed, in this hill country surrounding the town of Funchal, an alms-house which had been founded by Doña Maria Amelia, Empress of Brazil, which by the beauty of its situation and surroundings and the hospitality it dispensed attracted the visitors to the island. It was run by the Sisters of St. Vincent of Paul and two priests of the Mission.[1] The chaplains having fallen ill, M. Portal had been appointed to help, but he was pressed to stay longer than was strictly necessary, not only because of his health, but also (though he would never admit it) because of his good influence with the sisters.

At about the same time [2] Lord and Lady Halifax came

---

[1] *I.e.* Lazarists: see *supra*, p. 6, footnote.—A. T. M.

[2] It was, in fact, the end of December; see Lord Halifax's *Leo XIII and Anglican Orders*, p. 8.—A. T. M.

to Madeira with one of their sons whose bad health they hoped would benefit from the warm climate. They paid a long visit to the House, meeting the three priests of the Mission, and in the course of the conversation Lord Halifax got speaking to M. Portal, who writes: 'He asked me whether I would be willing to have an occasional talk with him on religious questions'. Of the first meeting, which was to have such far-reaching consequences, M. Portal writes:

I shall never forget the walks we took, along a winding path, right by the shore, towards *Camino nove*. It was almost wholly devoted to reconnoitering in unknown country. One knows the pleasure of the first attempts to make contact with a sympathetic soul. As usual I allowed the Englishman first say. He spoke most ably, covering the ground with extreme clarity. My turn came next, and although I employed neither his subtlety nor skill, I knew for certain that I was talking to a man of the highest intelligence as well as of wide and sound learning, but above all a big-hearted man. In this Anglican layman dwelt the soul of an apostle, full of love for Our Saviour Jesus Christ and ever seeking to promote his Master's glory.

Thus there began, quite unpremeditated, conversations which were to last several weeks, under the encouragement and blessing of the Bishop of Funchal, Monsignor Barreto. The parties have left us no details of these talks. M. Portal has merely said that the principal subject was Our Lord and the Church, and that the unhappy divisions separating those who claimed to be disciples of Jesus Christ was a subject to which their thoughts most often returned. The nature of the subjects and the depths of the arguments put forward during these walks inevitably led to their more profound examination. 'Our souls', writes M. Portal, 'seemed to intermingle into closer union.' Their common spirituality and the similarity of their outlook and hopes gradually built up a lifelong and unbreakable friendship which was destined to beget an even greater work.

Looking back on his own mental equipment at the date he landed in Madeira, M. Portal writes:

Such studies as I had made enabled me to talk on equal terms with the distinguished man I had so unexpectedly met. During four years I had been teaching dogmatic theology, and for some time I had been studying history, especially the history of the French Church, which had always greatly interested me. More recently I had carefully noted all that had been written of the chief characters of the nineteenth century, and about our catholic movement which characterized that period. This reading had given me a great love for the Church and desire to serve her, as well as introducing me to many great examples from whom much could be learned. I could therefore converse intelligently on these subjects; but I held very hazy ideas on the Anglican Church. Along with many others I thought of England as a Protestant country. As to their ordinations, all I knew was what was in two or three lines in our theological text books, which stated that they were doubtful. Otherwise I was quite ignorant, and on these subjects I found Lord Halifax a first-rate teacher.

The strong influence exercised by Lord Halifax on the mind of the young priest was due partly to their difference in age — Halifax was 50, Portal 34 — and partly to the fact that the former had, for many years past, played an active part in the religious controversies then taking place in England.

Charles Lindley Wood, the future Lord Halifax, was born on 7 June 1839, and educated at Eton and Christ Church, Oxford. At the age of 17 he was one of a party which accompanied the Prince of Wales on a tour to the continent, and later, on the Prince's marriage in 1863, he was appointed a Groom of the Bedchamber. His own marriage, in 1869, to Lady Agnes Courtenay — the daughter of one of the oldest titled families of England — and his prospect of a seat in the House of Lords when his father should die, seemed to mark him out for a brilliant political career. Moreover, his high ideals were worthy of his ancestry. In 1870, a little more than a year after his marriage and when his first child was but a few weeks old, he went to

France with the Red Cross volunteers to give help to the French prisoners of war (of the Franco-Prussian war) and by the middle of September he arrived in Sedan. In 1877, much against his personal inclination, he felt in duty bound to resign his post in the Prince's household, owing to the important part he was taking in the Church of England's struggle for her spiritual rights, which had then taken on a new aspect. In its first phase, the object of the 'Oxford Movement' had been to restore the ancient doctrines and principles which had for long been forgotten or ignored, and also to uphold the Church's independence of the civil authority. But now the struggle had shifted to the parishes whose priests, known as 'ritualists', were trying to introduce reforms into the public worship, and especially into the celebration of the Eucharist. Members of the 'Low Church', with their greater leanings towards Protestantism, did not hesitate to stir up disturbances in church during public worship, or to start proceedings in the courts against clergy guilty of innovations in the services. The continued presence in the Prince of Wales's household of Charles Wood (as he then was) could not have failed to be embarrassing in view of his prominent part in these religious struggles. But once freed from all such ties and political ambitions, the future Lord Halifax entered on a course in which, in all human probability, he would find, as M. Portal later said, 'little glory, many worries, but also much good to accomplish'.

In 1868 Lord Halifax (then the Hon. Charles Wood) had been elected, at the age of 28, President of the English Church Union. This society, which had been founded in 1860 with the general purpose of [1] implementing the teaching

---

[1] The objects of the English Church Union, as laid down in the constitution, were:
(1) To defend and maintain unimpaired the doctrine and discipline of the Church of England.
(2) In general, so to promote the interests of religion as to be, by God's help, a lasting witness in the land for the advancement of His glory and the good of His Church.
(3) To afford counsel and protection to all persons, lay or clerical, suffering under unjust aggression or hindrance in spiritual matters.—A. T. M.

13

of the Tractarians, by the end of the century had some 35,000 members, including thirty bishops and many thousands of the clergy. Its annual meeting was reckoned as one of the important events in English church life, and the President's speech as a manifesto and call to action. As President, Lord Halifax devoted himself, body and soul, to its work, and his speeches were regarded as the living voice of the catholic revival. Nor were his interests merely parochial, but embraced the whole Church: for instance in 1880 he wrote, on behalf of the English Church Union, to Cardinal Guibert, Archbishop of Paris, to convey their sympathy and dismay at the news of the expulsion of the religious orders from France.

We cannot remain silent when we learn that convents are ravaged, their chapels desecrated, and men known for their piety and good works thrown on the street. . . . We are completely with them in their resistance in defence of the sacred cause of religion.

The direction of his thoughts is seen in his early appreciation of the aspiration towards religious unity beginning to be felt in England, and his decision to give expression to it. Thus in 1880 Lord Halifax stated publicly the need to complete the catholic revival, and the impossibility of doing so fully without reunion with the Roman See.

There is one direction above all others towards which our eyes must ever be turning, in the hope that at last it may please God to allow us to see the first streaks of that dawning day which shall restore us to visible communion with the rest of the Latin Church, from which we have now been separated since the schism of the sixteenth century. [*Church Times*, 14 May 1880.]

Again at the annual meeting on 10 June 1885 he said:

union among themselves, and the restoration of the visible unity with the members of the Church abroad, east and west alike, but, above all, with the great Apostolic See of the West, with the Holy Roman Church, which had done so much to guard the true faith — these surely should be their objects and the objects nearest their hearts. [*The Times*, 11 June 1885.]

Finally in his speech at the 27th anniversary meeting of the English Church Union he made quite clear what were his hopes :

After all, if a central authority is good for the Anglican Communion, a central authority must be good for the Church at large. . . .

Can we at least conceive anything more conducive to the unity of the Church than such a common centre, provided always that the principle of centralization be so accepted as not to infringe on the right of local jurisdiction ? Certainly those who are willing to recognize an appeal from the Archbishop of Canterbury to the Judicial Committee need not scruple at an appeal to a Christian Bishop. Is there a single instructed Christian who would not prefer Leo XIII to the Privy Council ?

These passages, chosen from many more, show clearly the extent to which Lord Halifax's views had acquired definiteness when he first met M. Portal. Even before their talks in Madeira, he had decided on the direction of his religious work.

One can imagine what a revelation it was to M. Portal to listen to Lord Halifax's accounts of his twenty years' struggle for the catholic revival in his Church, and, if possible, for her reconciliation with Rome. In listening to him, M. Portal learned much, not least admiration for the integrity and piety of his new friend.

It was only natural that a conscientious priest like M. Portal, for whom Lord Halifax had formed such an obvious friendship, should feel a certain sorrow that so intelligent and good a Christian was outside the body of the catholic church. Lord Halifax guessed what his young friend felt, and in May 1890, just before they parted, wrote to him, 'Pray for me sometimes, that I be not one of those who, knowing the truth, fail to follow it'. Soon afterwards, writing from Italy, M. Portal referred directly to his hopes for Lord Halifax's conversion, and as some time passed without any answer, wrote again, ending his letter, 'Write to me to Paris, rue de Sèvres, 95, and tell me that my last letter did not annoy you'. To which Lord Halifax answered, 'Why should you think that your last letter annoyed me? I assure you that the reverse was the case, and that I am grateful for your many kindnesses to me. I quite understand your very proper hopes for me, but you know my position as regards them.' This position M. Portal did not then understand, though he soon came to do so.

It is stated clearly in a letter Lord Halifax wrote to his friend the Dean of Durham,[1] in January 1894, in which he compares Dr. Newman with Dr. Pusey, the second volume of whose life he had just read. He writes:

It is impossible to blame Dr. Newman. . . . Dr. Newman wanted a theory which should completely justify his own position, one which should make that position intellectually complete and secure. . . . I am compelled to admit that, humanly speaking, there was much to be said for the course he took, and yet, though I say this, I have also the feeling that what was not revealed to the wise and prudent was revealed to the childlike simplicity and goodness of Dr. Pusey; that events have justified Dr. Pusey's estimate of the situation and condemned Dr. Newman's. . . . Certainly our existing scandals are deplorable, and I have no sympathy with Anglican narrowness. I think it unjust, in view of our own conduct and history, to accuse the adherents of the Roman Church of being in schism in England. *There is a schism* with much blame on both sides; but to talk as many Anglicans do on this subject is in my opinion grossly unfair, inconsistent with historical fact, and contrary to justice and common-sense. But, having said all this, I have also to say that I am thankful to be where I am. We have a great work before us. How great we shall only know hereafter, and meanwhile to despair or be discouraged seems to me the height of ingratitude and faithlessness to Almighty God, who has so wonderfully helped us and blessed us hitherto.[2]

The friendship between Lord Halifax and M. Portal was close enough for them to talk freely to each other, and the latter's failure in the matter of Lord Halifax's conversion in

[1] The Very Reverend William Charles Lake.—A. T. M.
[2] *Memorials of William Charles Lake*, edited by Katharine Lake, 1901, pp. 314-315.—A. T. M.

no way upset their relationship. M. Portal has left us a statement of his reasons for continuing this close friendship which rather astonished some devout souls who could not be satisfied with anything short of individual conversion.

I soon realized that, humanly speaking, conversion was out of the question in the case of a man with such firm beliefs, and I continued a relationship which some people considered without purpose because I thought that individual conversion is not the only good one can achieve. It is equally important to try to understand the other's points of view and to overcome prejudices, especially when that other is highly influential in his own church.

To the friendship thus begun in Madeira each party brought his particular contribution. During the first talks Lord Halifax rather played the part of elder brother. He was the senior by sixteen years, and his great experience of men and events had given him a broader outlook than was then M. Portal's, whom he initiated into an understanding of the English religious world. However, the younger man had an open and receptive mind ; was extremely intelligent and endowed with great clarity of judgment : in addition he had a sound basis of theology and a practical experience of human beings, their problems and hopes. M. Portal, the devoted Catholic priest, already matured by pastoral experience and personal ill health, he too discovers and comes to love this lay apostle, like him burning with desire to serve Christ and His Church.

In many respects very different, these two were drawn to each other by a quality which each possessed to a rare degree ; a generous heart, quick to bestir itself for any great cause, and yet stable and controlled in their enthusiasm. Above all, each was essentially a simple character, free from all trace of *amour-propre*, completely sincere and honest — a kind of inner *naïveté*, which enabled each to read the other's thoughts.

M. Portal left Madeira in May 1890 ; and soon after, in July, Lord Halifax returned to England.

CHAPTER 3

Campaign for the Reunion of the Churches — Anglican Orders

LORD HALIFAX and M. Portal parted in Madeira, with 'a sort of presentiment that their meetings were not ended', but without any definite plan of action. These meetings were destined to have consequences other than the mere pleasure of private friendship.

M. Portal went from Madeira to Lisbon to attend to the affairs of his Order. He was chosen to accompany Mgr. Barreto, the Bishop of Funchal, on his journey to Rome. He greatly enjoyed his first visits to the places they passed through — Geneva, Naples, Loretto, Assisi, Florence, Bologna, Padua, Venice, Milan, and Turin — also the three weeks in Rome, the centre of Christianity, and his first meeting with Pope Leo XIII, who received him in private audience on the eve of his departure. Writing to Lord Halifax from Venice in July 1890, he said:

In Rome I had the joy of attending a meeting of the consistory, and especially of being received by the Pope. Leo XIII surprised me by his remarkable memory, as well as by his lively intelligence and quick mind. He referred to events connected with our Order which happened twenty years ago, giving full details as well as the names of the participants.

Although the memory of Lord Halifax was fresh in his mind, M. Portal felt no presentiment that in a few years he would again see, in very different circumstances, the Pontiff who was then granting him this short interview. On his return to Paris towards the end of July, M. Portal was sent, on account of his health, on a preaching mission to Spain.

It was while there that he learnt of the death of Lord Halifax's son, on account of whose health they had come to Madeira. The two friends exchanged letters full of Christian fortitude.

M. Portal wrote (14 October 1890) :

My dear friend, what a trial for you and Lady Halifax! Your loving heart was surely broken! God knows how dreadful is death when it strikes down those whom we love. You have lived too long and suffered too much not to have said sometimes, with St. Paul, *me toedet vivere*; and if death were to come to you, you would die as a true Christian, with little fear or regret. But to lose one's children. In my ministry I can, by God's grace, reconcile people to their own death, but I have never succeeded in comforting a bereaved father or mother.

There is but one comforter, the God of Calvary and suffering ; and remember that Jesus willed that a mother should be at the foot of the Cross. In your own sorrow you can recite the noble lines of the *Stabat Mater Dolorosa*. I will ever pray for you. Yesterday I said Mass for your dear child, with many prayers for yourself, and will continue doing so. My dear friend, I would so like to be with you at this sad time. I am sure that you are surrounded by good friends, but feel it a loss not being able to express my sympathy in person.

With this letter he sent to Lady Halifax a small book by the Abbé Perrauld,[1] which was then very popular. When the Duke of Clarence died, in 1892, Lord Halifax in turn presented it to the Princess of Wales. Later M. Portal wrote :

About ten years ago I too came near to starting on the long journey of no return, since when the uncertain state of my health has often reminded me that I might be struck down at any moment. This was good for me. I have, unfortunately, had practical experience of the truth that 'the more one walks the dirtier one gets', but at least I have thus acquired a certain detachment which helps my religious life. Surely life, real life, is to love God as much as one can in spite of a growing coldness

---

[1] *Méditations de l'abbé Perrauld.*—A. T. M.

of heart, and to do good (much good) to others, and on the journey to gather a few flowers in the shape of friends.

In answer Lord Halifax wrote [1] (14 November 1890) :

> Our Lord has been so good to us that it would be the basest ingratitude not to accept what comes from Him fully trusting that it is the best, both for ourselves and for our dear ones. I try to do so. In any case it is not hard to believe that our Lord knows best what in the long run is for our good. If trials be necessary, one should try to accept them joyfully.
>
> When one thinks of one's sins, it would be frightening to experience only the joys of life. One would feel deserted, as if beyond hope.

After his preaching mission in Spain, M. Portal was appointed treasurer of the large seminary at Cahors, and at once reminded Lord Halifax of his promise to make a retreat with him if he were ever to go back to a seminary. But family bereavements and illnesses, as well as his numerous commitments, ecclesiastical, political, and social, left Lord Halifax little time to arrange meetings with M. Portal. It was the latter who, in 1891, spent a week of his holidays with his friend and his family at Roscoff, where he met, for the first time, Lord Halifax's son, Edward.[2]

M. Portal's position at the seminary at Cahors, first as treasurer, and shortly afterwards as professor of moral theology, gave him opportunities for making a close study of the history of the English schism, and generally of the problem of the reunion of the separated Churches. He was interested in the Greek no less than in the English Church. He made full use of these opportunities, and put in a great deal of study in the peaceful surroundings at Cahors. He read not only the great classical works, but also the more modern, even the quite recent ones, of which his friend told him; among others the Russian Khomiakoff's *The Latin Church*

---

[1] In fact this letter from Lord Halifax was written before he received the one from M. Portal last mentioned : see *Leo XIII and Anglican Orders*, by Lord Halifax, pp. 45-47.—A. T. M.

[2] The first Earl of Halifax, died 23 December 1959.—A. T. M.

and Protestantism, the Reverend Aubrey Moore's *Defence of Anglican Orders*, and the Abbé Duchesne's *Les Origines du culte chrétien*.

It was not in M. Portal's nature to remain, for very long, engrossed in academic study without seeking to give it practical expression. It seemed to him that the most helpful approach was to try to interest catholic opinion in France in the events then taking place in the English Church. M. Portal writes to Lord Halifax in November 1890 :

> I am more than ever convinced that good could come from our being informed of the conditions in your Church. Reunion, if God so wills it, cannot come suddenly : much preparation is necessary in both communions. Let us put all our efforts into working for this glorious consummation, by scattering a grain here and there, leaving to God to raise up the harvest in His good time.

Every kind of suggestion as to the subjects to be dealt with in the French Press sprang from M. Portal's fertile imagination — Cardinal Newman, on the occasion of his proposed statue ; the ecclesiastical congress held in Wales ; the re-establishment of religious orders. . . . None of these directly affected the problem of reunion : it was merely hoped to interest and inform French public opinion of the religious conditions of the English. M. Portal was fully aware of the French character, its quickness to respond to and popularize any really great cause. In January 1892 he writes to Lord Halifax :

> I have heard say that we French are commercial travellers in other people's ideas. It is certain that we are, by nature, popularizers and advocates. You should take advantage of this peculiarity of ours and tell us of the state of your Church. If it interested them you can be sure that all would hear of it.

When M. Portal speaks of a 'long campaign', he means especially that both sides should stop ignoring one another.

The light will perhaps shine one day. In any case may our Lord bless our efforts, and grant that, by His grace, the small seed sown in friendship in the field of His Church, may one day bring forth the fruit of unity.

However, none of the projected articles appeared. Lord Halifax was much too busy to write, despite M. Portal's scoldings.

We must get you out of that indifference which you say, makes even your most necessary duties seem impossible.

Meanwhile M. Portal was at work, and a passage he happened to come on, while preparing a course of lectures on moral theology, decided him on the steps he should take. In the same letter to Lord Halifax he writes :

I had occasion to consult Mgr. Cecconi's History of the Vatican Council, which I did not know before and in which I have been absorbed for the last two days. Naturally I began with what concerns your church, and I can hardly say how very interested I was in some extracts from a pamphlet by Cobb,[1] 'A few Words . . .', and by the suggestion of a Bollandist, Father de Buck, particularly in his very charitable as well as learned letter to the Church Times. There is here material for long talks, but for the moment I would call attention to some words of Cobb ; 'We profess on the other hand to be in possession of documentary evidence amply sufficient to reverse this traditionary verdict (on Anglican Orders). Yet what have we done to lay it before them and obtain a reversal?'[2] Along with Cobb I ask you, Have you taken any steps to put these proofs before your adversaries? Your Church should publish a thesis proving decisively that your orders are valid, which, if not an official publication, should be written by one of your most learned theologians. And why not take advantage of the present pontificate? Leo XIII is a broad-minded and conciliatory man, who would, I am sure, examine most carefully both the opportuneness of raising the question and the question itself. As Cobb writes, Rome is anyhow your patriarchal centre, to whom a dispute should be brought for decision. Believe me, my dear friend, this will

[1] Gerald Cobb, 'A few words on Reunion and the coming Council at Rome', London, 1869.—A. T. M.
[2] Cobb, *op. cit.* p. 16.

always remain the first question to be resolved; and it is an easier one in that the answer depends on questions of fact, not of faith. To bring forward the question would be, I think, a great step, as it would mark the opening of negotiations, and in this, as in so much else, it is the first step that counts.

This letter marks a turning-point in the life of M. Portal. His ardent wish for the union of the Churches had been growing throughout the years, but he had been uncertain as to the methods to be employed. How could be brought about both in England and France, a movement so strong as to be able to shake up the great ecclesiastical bodies, separated for nearly four centuries, and bring them to a frame of mind in which they would seek to know and to understand each other better? But from now on he uses the question of the validity of Anglican Orders as a method of stimulating learned works and friendly meetings between theologians of the two Churches.

M. Portal was so carried away by this new idea that he seems to have forgotten that only quite recently he had em- phasized the need for a long exploratory approach. Lord Halifax, with his greater appreciation of the situation in England, doubted the wisdom of his friend's suggestion that the Anglican bishops should ask Rome to hold an enquiry into the validity of their Orders. He writes (29 January 1892):

The state of mind of both sides makes me fear that, at the moment, no good would come of such a request. A more hopeful approach would be for the Archbishop of Canterbury to ask the Pope to allow English representatives free access to the Vatican Library and all the archives of the Roman Court.

I was talking about this the other day to the Bishop of Rochester;[1] and I think that if it were thought that such a request would not be refused, it might well be made. Assuming that the problems of etiquette and titles could be arranged satis- factorily, the establishment of personal contacts between the

[1] The Right Reverend Randall Thomas Davidson, subsequently Bishop of Winchester and Archbishop of Canterbury.

Archbishop of Canterbury and the Holy See would be highly important.

But M. Portal stuck to his opinion as to the priority of the question of Orders. On 3 February 1892 he wrote to Lord Halifax :

The question of Orders is ever and necessarily the first one to be examined. Mgr. Cecconi has written, that 'all catholics, including, I make bold to say, the Holy Father himself, would be glad to embark on a frank and learned discussion of a subject on which Mr. Cobb has expressed such definite views. This would greatly benefit not only historical science, but also the salvation of souls, as it would finally close a three centuries old historical-dogmatic controversy'.

M. Portal entertained no doubt that Rome's attitude would be friendly.

I do not think [he writes in the same letter] that Rome would require, as a condition precedent to examining the question, subscription to the whole Roman teaching : hence it could be discussed apart from doctrinal questions.

The enthusiasm of the two friends was kept up by a lively correspondence in which were mixed up accounts of Lord Halifax's domestic trials with every kind of theological and historical consideration.

Lady Halifax's health had remained weak after the death of her eldest son, and in consequence the family paid visits to different watering-places — Roscoff in 1891, Mont-Dore in 1892 and 1893. During these M. Portal was able to pay short visits to his friends, and deepen the intimacy in which he found such solace. Of all these meetings, that which gave the two friends the most pleasure was the week's visit which Lord Halifax paid to M. Portal at the seminary at Cahors in the beginning of April 1892. The budding young ecclesiastics were much surprised when this stranger — a layman, English and an Anglican — came to stay for a whole week. The Abbé Calvet, who was a student at the time, writes, 'Great was our surprise to see the obvious piety of this *heretic*: a surprise which did us much good'.

The project of some publications on Anglican Orders was fully discussed and developed during the conversations at Cahors (1892) and Mont-Dore (1892 and 1893): each side was to produce its own work. At the same time contact was made with the new Archbishop of Westminster, His Eminence Cardinal Vaughan, for neither Lord Halifax nor M. Portal had any thought of keeping the English catholics outside the movement: on the contrary they hoped for their co-operation. At first the Cardinal was favourably inclined, and promised to support any request which might be made to the Vatican for permission to search the archives. No agreement was reached, however, on the method of approach, either to the question of Anglican Orders or the more general one of reunion. The Cardinal's mind was made up on this: he said that the question of Rome was the crucial one which would have to be settled in the end, and that it was therefore better to begin with it. The promoters of reunion did not agree at all. They were undertaking a work which would take a long time, and could only hope to succeed in an atmosphere of mutual respect and good will. This they hoped to foster by arranging meetings at which the teachings and practices of the Churches could be fully explained. This seemed to them a more promising approach than starting straight off with the Roman question.

The resuscitation of the question of Anglican Orders seemed to increase rather than diminish the antagonism between Anglicans and English Roman Catholics. In August 1893 Cardinal Vaughan preached on the subject, provoking a reply by Archbishop Benson during his pastoral visit at Ashford.[1] Cardinal Newman's old remark that it was easier to find in France an atmosphere favourable to working for reunion was proved very true.

In view of the determined opposition of Cardinal Vaughan, soon to become that of many well-known Roman

[1] The *Guardian*, 8 November 1893.

Catholics, Lord Halifax and M. Portal had to decide whether to abandon a long-cherished project or to continue with it, in spite of the threat, which was more serious than they first thought. They decided to continue.

The question of the validity of Anglican Orders involves consideration of the legislation of the time of Elizabeth I. In 1559 Parliament passed, first the Act of Supremacy, which gave to the Queen the title 'Supreme Governor' of both Church and State, and restored to her the powers formerly vested in Henry VIII and Edward VI; and secondly a new Act of Uniformity which reintroduced the Book of Common Prayer of 1552,[1] and which imposed on all ecclesiastical and lay officials an oath binding them to an observance of the Act of Supremacy.[2] There was also a publication of a new set of Articles [3] of Religion, reduced in number from forty-two to thirty-nine.

The fifteen bishops then existing had opposed both Acts, and all but one refused to take the oath and were deprived. Accordingly the Queen had to chose enough bishops to reconstitute the episcopal bench. For Archbishop of Canterbury she chose Matthew Parker, who was elected Archbishop of Canterbury by the Canterbury Chapter on 1 August 1559. He was consecrated on 17 December 1559 by Barlow, Bishop of Bath and Wells, and three other bishops, according to the rites of the Edwardian Ordinal. Parker later consecrated thirteen [4] other bishops, and so became the stem from whom derives the English episcopate subsequent to Elizabeth I. Two questions arise on this: (1) Was Barlow, Parker's consecrator, a true bishop? (2) If the answer to the first question be 'Yes', was Parker's consecration by Barlow a valid consecration?

---

[1] In fact this Book contained some slight but important changes from that of 1552.—A. T. M.

[2] This is incorrect, as the oath was imposed by the Act of Supremacy itself.—A. T. M.

[3] The Articles were drawn up by Convocation in 1563, being finally ratified by the Queen in 1571.—A. T. M.

[4] The number was, in fact, eleven: see Frere, *English Church in Reigns of Elizabeth and James I*, pp. 48-49.—A. T. M.

There had been frequent controversy between Catholic and Anglican theologians on the validity of Anglican Orders. Although Father Courayeu, a Canon Regular of St. Geneviève, had in 1723 published a dissertation upholding their validity, the majority of Catholic theologians regarded them as not only irregular but invalid. And the practice in Rome, requiring clergy of the Anglican Church converted to Rome to be re-ordained, accorded with this view. M. Portal was also well acquainted with the case of John Gordon, in 1704, in which Rome decided that his Anglican Orders were invalid 'by reason of defect of intention and insufficiency of form used by the heretical Anglicans'. But he believed that the further studies of the theological doctrine of the intention necessary in the minister of the sacraments to render them valid, as well as the historical researches of Anglican scholars, made the decision capable of being reopened. In any case he was more concerned with creating opportunities for contacts between scholars of the two communions in the hope of creating a wish for reunion on both sides. He regarded the outlook as most favourable, as is seen from his letter to Lord Halifax of 5 June 1893, commenting on an address recently given by Mgr. Langenieux [1] on the Eastern Church :

This idea of unity is in everybody's mind. It is the wind blowing, or rather beginning to blow gently. We must make the most of it and remember, especially, that there is not only the Eastern Church to bring in, but that, nearer to hand, the Island of the Saints is struggling manfully to rid itself of a thousand political and other fetters.

In this wind M. Portal saw the breath of the Holy Spirit, which has never ceased to inspire the Church, and himself started on his work.

In January 1894, using the pen-name of Fernand Dalbus, M. Portal published, in France, his pamphlet on Anglican Orders. This, in forty-seven pages, is a very concentrated study. It covers important questions regarding the rite of

[1] Archbishop of Rheims.—A. T. M.

Holy Orders and the Anglican Ordinal; whether Barlow and Parker were ever in fact consecrated bishops, and also what must be presumed to have been the intention of Barlow when he consecrated Parker, and of Parker in the consecrations he administered later.

That Barlow (bishop elect of St. Asaph in 1536, but translated to Bath and Wells in the same year, and subsequently to Chichester) was, *in fact*, consecrated is pretty firmly established. He must have been consecrated in June 1536, after his appointment to Bath and Wells. It is true that the official record is missing, but so it is in the case of many contemporary bishops whom no one questions. Further, it is to be noted that Barlow took his seat as Bishop of Bath and Wells in the House of Lords on 15 June 1536, which by the House's Standing Orders he could do only on producing documentary proof of consecration. Finally he joined in consecrations in 1539 and 1542, which the English Ordinal restricts to consecrated bishops. Barlow's consecration of Parker is completely proved by the official records, still extant. At the invitation of the English Archbishop Abbot, in 1614, they were examined by Catholic representatives, and the record of this examination still exists. The Nag's Head story, that Parker's supposed consecration had taken place in a tavern as a masquerade, was still current, but was regarded as a monstrous calumny by all responsible historians. As Canon Estcour wrote, 'It is a great pity that the Nag's Head story was ever put forward seriously, for it is so absurd that the only result has been that people have questioned the good faith of catholic theologians in their objections to Anglican Orders'. That Barlow and Parker were *in fact* consecrated must be taken as proved.

The question then arises whether Parker's consecration was a valid one, making necessary an examination of the rite; the words Barlow spoke and his intention in speaking them, and generally whether the alterations made in the ceremony of consecration were such as to invalidate it. These were all difficult questions, the more so since fairly widely differing forms of consecration have existed in the Church throughout the centuries. In 1549 and again in 1552 the English Reformers had substituted a revised Ordinal for the old English Pontificals. It is commonly held by modern theologians — as taught by De Augustinis — that for episcopal consecration the only essential matter is the laying on of hands and the only form a eucharistic or consecratory prayer. The words of the prayer vary in different catholic liturgies, but its tenor is always the same : it invokes God's blessing on the ordinand and asks that he may be given grace to carry out the duties of his office. As in the English Ordinal this prayer, which follows immediately after the *Veni Creator*, is very similar to that in the medieval (pre-Reformation) Sarum Pontifical, and is followed by the imposition of hands with an invocation of the Holy Ghost, M. Portal thought that the traditional rite had been sufficiently preserved. The weakness of this argument lies in the absence of any such clear reference to the priestly power to offer sacrifice as might determine the somewhat vague language of the consecratory prayer. However, a comparison of the Anglican form with those used in many earlier catholic ordinals as well as the present Greek Church suggests that no enumeration of the priestly powers is indispensable, and that the efficacity of the form of words derives primarily from its being a prayer.

Another difficult question is as to the intention of the minister of the sacrament to 'do what the Church does'. Theologians are at one in thinking that the orthodoxy of the minister's beliefs is not essential to the validity of the sacrament, if, using a sufficient form, he intends, in the words of Eugenius IV, to do what the Church does — *intentio faciendi quod facit Ecclesia*. M. Portal states very fairly the arguments for and against the view (a view put forward especially by English Catholics) that the Church of England does not intend to make real priests, *i.e.* ministers who offer the Eucharistic sacrifice. In this connection he draws attention to the fact that certain of the Church of England's statements,

which seem at first sight to deny that the mass is in any
sense a sacrifice, are really aimed at the opinions advanced
by some medieval theologians and not at the true catholic
doctrine. He writes:

> At that time (the Reformation) some very strange views, now
> quite repudiated by catholics, were put forward and defended by
> theologians of no mean repute. For instance it was said that the
> eucharistic sacrifice was a complete, absolute sacrifice, expiatory
> independently of our Lord's sacrifice on the Cross. People dared
> to say that our Lord's sacrifice on the Cross was an expiation for
> original sin, for sins committed under the Old Law, and for indi-
> vidual sins before baptism, whereas the mass operated as the
> expiation of sins committed after baptism. It was also said that
> mortal sins were wiped out by the sacrifice of the mass, *ex opere
> operato*.

This largely explains the rather brutish terms of Article 31[1]
of the English 39 Articles.

It is clear, therefore, that the question, 'What did the
authors of the Prayer Book intend?' is difficult to answer
with any degree of certainty. It is not merely the interpretation of a book which must be sought, but a whole intellectual and religious atmosphere of a distant period to be
recovered. Few could claim complete success in doing this.

The Roman Church would agree that, even though the
English Church held heretical views on the sacrament of
Orders, her ordinations and consecrations, assuming the
sufficiency of the rite, would be valid, because the wrong
beliefs of the minister of the sacrament must not be confused
with his intention. The latter is a function of the will, not
necessarily invalidated by intellectual error. It would be
otherwise if, as a result of wrong beliefs, the English Bishops
'deliberately limited their intention . . . *e.g.* by saying, "I

---

[1] This Article reads as follows: 'The Offering of Christ once made is that
perfect redemption, propitiation, and satisfaction, for all the sins of the whole
world, both original and actual; and there is none other satisfaction for sin,
but that alone. Wherefore the sacrifices of Masses, in which it was commonly
said, that the Priest did offer Christ for the quick and the dead, to have
remission of pain or guilt, were blasphemous fables, and dangerous deceits.'
—A. T. M.

ordain you a priest, but I do not give you power to conse-
crate". . . . But such a limitation is not to be presumed;
it must be expressly proved.' It looked, therefore, as though
M. Portal would, as regards intention, come down favourably to Anglican Orders.

Unfortunately considerable Calvinistic influences operated
on the minds of the English theologians and bishops who
produced the Prayer Book of 1552, which expunged the
name 'mass', and minimized the sacrificial character at the
expense of the purely commemorative aspect of Holy Communion.   In regard to the sacraments, Barlow wished to
return to the theology of the primitive Church, but his theological teaching, as well as that of Bucer, Cranmer, and most
of the Reformers, was completely contrary to that of either
the primitive or contemporary Church.   In view of his
denial that Holy Orders were a Sacrament, it seemed to M.
Portal incredible that Barlow had not, when consecrating,
a definite positive intention not to confer any power to
offer sacrifice.   Accordingly in spite of the arguments that
the English Church had a general intention to preserve the
Orders mentioned in the New Testament, he was unable
to regard Barlow's intention when he consecrated Parker
as other than doubtful — a doubt affecting, of course, all
Anglican Orders.   Later Cardinal Gaspari came to the same
conclusion and for the same reasons.

In the last part of his pamphlet M. Portal turns from
episcopal consecration to the ordinations of priests, and
points out that the Ordinal[1] of Edward VI abolished the
porrectio instrumentorum, an essential matter of ordination.   It
follows that the first English bishops never validly ordained
any priest, and so there could be no continuance of the
episcopate, for want of an apt subject for consecration.   It
is true that the *porrectio instrumentorum*, still unknown in the
East, had only been in use in the West for a few centuries,
but the schoolmen had held it to be essential, a view

[1] The Ordinal attached to the Prayer Book of 1552 omitted the ceremony:
it was included in the Ordinal attached to the 1549 Prayer Book.—A. T. M.

sanctioned by Eugenius IV in his 'Decretum de Unione Armeniorum'.[1] It followed, therefore, that the Church of England has no valid Orders.

This argument raised a new point, and it was quite definitely rejected by distinguished theologians and by Mgr. Duchesne, the historian. These gave opinions that Anglican Orders are valid, though of course no one imagined that Rome would give official recognition to this view. As Mgr. Duchesne wrote,[2] the Church is always 'tutiorist' in regard to the sacraments.

The immediate interest roused by this pamphlet from the pen of a young and little-known priest — the Archbishops of Canterbury and York studied it closely — seemed to show that the time was opportune to raise the question. And it was written in a spirit of friendship and charity, unlike the writings of others : as Mr. Denny [3] wrote to Lord Halifax, 'the spirit in which he writes is so different, so much more in accordance, if I may say so, with that of our common Lord and Master'.

M. Portal's pamphlet ended with an eloquent appeal for unity.

No longer, it seems, do we engage in fratricidal strife. In a world hostile to the teaching of our Lord and Saviour, His followers realize instinctively the need for closer union to support the coming struggle between believers and unbelievers. The Church herself plays her part in the great work for unity now going on in the world, and one can detect signs of a coming religious peace. Mgr. Strossmayer [4] has predicted that the 20th century will see the reunion of the Greek and Latin Churches. In England prejudices are disappearing, the Established Church asserts her independence of the civil authority, the influence of the Oxford Movement continues to grow, and the Church is

---

[1] The present Roman Catholic teaching is that the *porrectio instrumentorum* is not essential, so as to make its absence invalidate the ordination.—A. T. M.

[2] In a letter to M. Portal dated 13 April 1894 : see Halifax, *op. cit.* p. 80. —A. T. M.

[3] The Reverend Edward Denny, joint author, with Canon Lacey, of *De Hierarchia.*—A. T. M.

[4] Bishop of Dickovár.—A. T. M.

recovering the fullness of the faith. The inevitable, providential end of this evolution is Rome. This is dreaded by the Protestants, but many Anglicans wish for it. No catholic worthy of the name can do other than long for that blessed day; but when it will dawn is known to God alone.

Then, recapitulating the arguments set out above, he maintained that the question of Orders would have to come up for discussion at the outset of any negotiations between Catholics and Anglicans. But apart from necessity, he regarded this question as affording a subject eminently suitable for initiating negotiations. M. Portal felt sure that if once conversations on this point could be started, discussions and explanations of wider issues would come, and might finally result in agreement. This appears also to have been the view of Cardinal Wiseman, as is seen from his open letter to the Earl of Shrewsbury, dated 21 September 1841.

I have thus indirectly stated what would seem to be our first duty : to offer cheerfully and honestly every explanation in our power, and point out where our real doctrines are mistaken, where they are confounded with mere permissive practices, and where they may be liable to abuse. The sooner a clear and distinct understanding can be come to upon these matters, the better for the cause. . . . In his reply to the Pope, when consulted on the best method of reconciling the followers of the Confession of Augsburg with the Holy See, the learned Bishop (Bossuet) observes that Providence had allowed so much Catholic doctrine to be preserved in that Confession, that full advantage should be taken of the circumstance : that no *retractions* should be demanded, but an explanation of the Confession in accordance with Catholic doctrines.[1]

Lord Halifax, too, thought the same : on 11 July 1894, he writes to M. Portal :

The first thing necessary is that we know each other : the second that we really do want union with all our heart, and without making any sacrifices to truth, to judge as leniently as possible

---

[1] Cardinal Wiseman, 'A letter on Catholic Unity', pp. 33, 38.

all that has been said and done in the past or is being said and done now, by either side. Above all many explanations are needed. I feel quite sure that on such matters as the Sacraments, Purgatory, the Invocation of Saints, worship, confession and the priesthood, there exist no doctrinal differences between us as could not be reconciled if both sides were willing to explain themselves fully, and insist as necessary only on that which is *de fide*, leaving a latitude on other matters. . . . For example, if it were legitimate to interpret the definition of the Vatican Council in the sense that the Pope is *only infallible* when he speaks after having taken all proper means to inform himself of what the Church teaches, and that he is infallible only when he promulgates that which the Church teaches, I think reconciliation would be possible on a subject which, not long since, appeared quite incapable of adjustment. It is the same with other questions. But what is needed is that we get to know each other.

M. Portal was convinced that to secure such better knowledge between Catholics and Anglicans, conferences must be arranged, and this conviction he retained throughout all the difficulties and complications which ensued — indeed until the end of his life. On 24 January 1921, he writes to Cardinal Mercier :

The question of Holy Orders was chosen as providing a suitable meeting ground for Anglicans and Catholics, where they could discuss, not only the validity of Anglican Orders, but also other problems which separate them. As regards Holy Orders, there was agreement on certain basic principles : the need for uninterrupted transmission : of sufficiency of matter and form, and of an intention to do that which the Church does. I thought that there were sufficient points of contact to enable the question to be discussed profitably. It was not really necessary to come to any final decision on the validity of Anglican Orders : that could have been left to the end, after all the other problems had been discussed.

Such were, in 1894, the beliefs and hopes which were to guide M. Portal in his life's work.

*   *   *

Thinking that a visit to England would help to promote mutual understanding, M. Portal arranged to come and stay for three weeks from the end of July 1894, but on the way he stopped in Paris with a view to enlisting the help of some writers in putting out propaganda for his campaign. Thus he met Messrs. Levé, Tavernier, Arthur Loth, Henri Lorin, and the Abbé Boudinhon, who was professor of canon law at the Catholic Institute. He arrived in London on 30 July 1894 and was taken round Church circles by Lord Halifax. Thus he saw for himself the vigour of the catholic revival in the Church of England, showing itself both in the restoration of the liturgy, the cult of the Blessed Virgin Mary and the Saints, and also in the renovation of the religious life. He decided that on his return to France he would publish a short description of what was happening in England to enlighten the French public. Accompanied by Lord Halifax, he began a round of visits to the High Church parishes and Anglican religious communities. He [1] went to the churches of Saint Augustine, Kilburn, Saint Mary the Virgin, Graham Street, St. Agnes and St. John the Divine, Kennington, where he was struck by the great resemblance between the ritualist and catholic ceremonial. The sung mass of St. Matthew's Westminster was preceded by a litany of the Saints.

'After the service', writes M. Portal, 'I was taken to the presbytery and introduced to the vicar, Father Trevelyan. He and his assistant priests live in common and the house is so arranged as to be able to be used for retreats. We talked about my pamphlet and reunion.' This last sentence shows that, while informing himself of the state of religious life in England, M. Portal never lost sight of his primary purpose, viz. reunion. There seemed to him to exist such a fundamental similarity between the two Churches in their religious life and works of charity, as to make the scandal of disunity stand out more clearly, and he based great hopes for the future on the interest aroused and the prayers

[1] This account of his journey is taken largely from M. Portal's own diary.

everywhere promised. The religious communities were objects of great interest to M. Portal, who looked to find in them some measure of the catholic revival. He visited the Sisters of Mary, the St. Peter's Sisterhood, the Sisters of Bethany in Lloyd's Square, and the Priory at Ascot, where the old Superioress and Sister Clare had known Dr. Pusey, who used to go there for holidays and to rest. He has left a typical account of his visit to the house of the Sisters of Charity at Bristol.

Friday 3rd of August. We went to Bristol solely to visit the Sisters of Charity, called Sisters of St. Raphael. I was agreeably surprised to see in the sitting-room a portrait of St. Vincent of Paul. We were received by their warden, the Reverend Arthur Ward, and by the Sister Superior with great cordiality, which increased when I told them I was one of the family of St. Vincent. I was left alone with the Superioress (according to Lord Halifax, that I might hear her confessions) and we had a heart to heart talk. She told me that before establishing the community she had gone to Paris to visit both the mother house and several other houses of our Sisters of Charity. She still had the visiting card of the Superior General which she had used as a letter of introduction. She was doing her best to imitate our Sisters of Charity and showed me some books she had, among others one by Pistoye of which I was ignorant, and she asked me one or two questions about the rule. She also invited me to have a private interview with each Sister, which I had with apologies to decline. After lunch we went into the common living-room and engaged in general conversation. We spoke of St. Vincent and before leaving the Sisters asked me to say a few words about the Saint. This I did, taking as my text the words 'Love God with the sweat of your brow and the strength of your arm'. I ended by stressing the need for charity in their dealings with each other. I cannot express how greatly I was moved by my visit.

The second object of M. Portal's visit was to meet and confer with high dignitaries of the Church of England so as to be well-briefed to explain the situation to those in France, who would come to him for information. During his visit to Lambeth Palace he met the Bishop of Salisbury,[1] who had just returned from a long visit to Australia, and took the occasion to thank him for his letter which had appeared in the second edition of Dalbus's Pamphlet, answering most courteously and moderately that of Cardinal Bourret, Bishop of Rodez. The Bishop of Salisbury drew particular attention to the works of Forbes,[2] who was Bishop of Edinburgh in the seventeenth century.

At Cambridge M. Portal met the Reverend T. A. Lacey, the Reverend E. G. Wood, and Doctor Cunningham, and all discussed at length Dalbus's Pamphlet. Lord Halifax also introduced M. Portal to Dr. Mandell Creighton, Bishop of Peterborough, who invited them to stay the night at the Palace, where they were most graciously received by Mrs. Mandell Creighton. She guessed what would be a French priest's reaction to his first introduction to an English episcopal home, for she confided to Lord Halifax: 'What will the Abbé think when he meets a Bishop's wife, it really is rather ridiculous'. Lord Halifax used sometimes to say, jokingly, 'I would gladly burn all Bishop's wives'. M. Portal was most impressed by the Bishop with whom he had a long conversation. The latter spoke of the necessity of a serious study of history, as, in order to understand the doctrinal statements of the Church of England, it was necessary to be acquainted with the general theological position previous to the Council of Trent, and not to import into a judgment of what was said and done in the sixteenth century, considerations really determined by events and convictions belonging to a later period. The following dialogue then took place. M. Portal asked:

Does the Church of England recognize a primacy of the Bishop of Rome?

A certain primacy certainly, answered the Bishop.

---

[1] Dr. John Wordsworth.—A. T. M.

[2] William Forbes (1585–1634). He wrote a defence of the doctrine of the Real Presence, and though he criticized the doctrine of Transubstantiation, he denied that it was heretical.—A. T. M.

Would you admit that the Pope after taking all appropriate means to determine what is a true doctrine held by the Church, may infallibly proclaim it?

The Bishop assented.

In order that belief in such a doctrine should become *de fide*, would you regard it as necessary that a Church accept it?[1]

Not necessarily, said the Bishop.

Would you then agree that councils are only one means of determining the truth of which the Church is a repository?

Yes, answered the Bishop.

It gives me great pleasure, My Lord, to hear you express these views, for it seems to me that there is little between us on the question of infallibility.

To which the Bishop replied that he often told his own people that they did not understand what they were saying when they talked about the Pope.

M. Portal felt that his talk with the Bishop had shown him the lines on which to proceed in his future conversations, especially with the ecclesiastical authorities. At the close of the conversation the Bishop asked Lord Halifax if M. Portal had yet seen the Archbishop of Canterbury, adding, 'he must see the Archbishop'.

Before going to Canterbury, M. Portal and Lord Halifax stopped at York to visit the Archbishop,[2] who took the two friends into his study and opened the conversation by showing them the *Life of St. Charles Borromeo* and *Life of Mgr. Dupanloup*.

'I try', he said, 'to inspire myself with the spirit of St. Charles, and as for Monseigneur Dupanloup I have tried to organize my diocese on his model, and I think if he were in my place he would be able to govern it very much as he governed the diocese of Orleans, and would not find much difference.' Then the conversation turned to the question of union and the Archbishop asked M. Portal to speak quite

---

[1] There is a discrepancy between this account and that given by Lord Halifax in his *Leo XIII and Anglican Orders*, p. 97. The latter ends this sentence with the words 'by a formal act'.—A. T. M.

[2] Dr. Maclagan.

38

freely to him. M. Portal has left a written account of this interview.

I had a feeling that our interview might prove of considerable importance. The Archbishop's attitude was very sympathetic and he is obviously a man of deep spirituality. The atmosphere in which our small gathering took place was one of the godliness and love of the Church. Before beginning I prayed for God's help and that of my patron saints, and proceeded to talk sixteen to the dozen. The main subjects on which I dwelt were:

1. Our complete ignorance about the Church of England shown by our continual confusion of Anglicans with Protestants.

2. This ignorance is partly our fault but Anglicans are also to blame. Why do they not see to it that their position is known and why do they not disassociate themselves from the Protestants, especially in the foreign mission field?

3. The general movement towards union.

4. The goodwill of Leo XIII, also that of our papers, viz. Le Monde, L'Univers and Le Moniteur de Rome.

5. The need to make the most of the movement and of the Church of England to vindicate its position and its desire for union.

6. In France the general attention is now turned to the Eastern Churches. The need to emphasize that there exists another church just next door to us. From any standpoint Canterbury is nearer to Rome than to Constantinople.

7. The ardent wish for union now stirring the English church should be made known to us.

8. The present moment is especially opportune in view of the line taken by Leo XIII.

9. Finally the need to avoid controversial talk or writing.

The Archbishop seldom interrupted, on the contrary his friendly attitude greatly encouraged me. When I had finished he asked me what were the views of our Bishops, I answered that like the Pope they wished for union but that I knew of no particular views which any had. I laid great stress on the absolute necessity of making known to our Catholic people the history, the doctrine and the present condition of the church of England. The Archbishop spoke of the approach of Leo XIII to the Easterners, saying it was impossible not to be touched at the sight of this old man, like St. John, making this appeal to the charity of Christians. We were all profoundly moved, and the conversation ended with the Archbishop saying, 'Let us hope that we are assisting in the beginning of something really great in the interest of the Church.

When Lord Halifax and I left at half past five our eyes were dim with tears of emotion. He grasped my hand and said, 'My friend I don't want to flatter you but it was all perfect, I am sure that you felt, as I did, that God's blessing overshadowed our meeting.' On the journey back I reflected on the strange rôle I was playing, a rôle I had not forseen nor particularly desired. I have never been more sure that we were being used for some great purpose.

There remained a final visit to be made, that to the Primate of All England, the successor of St. Augustine, Archbishop of Canterbury, sometimes called the Pope of the second Rome (*Papa alterius Romae*). Benson is one of those men who, very conscious of the responsibility of their position, fear to say more than they ought and consequently often say a great deal less than is in their minds for fear of being misunderstood. Our reception was courteous.

When he was first asked to see us, he had said that he did not think he ought to receive a papal emissary which greatly amused both Lord Halifax and myself. I said to him very much what I had said to the Archbishop of York. Throughout, the Archbishop of Canterbury seemed to be adopting the attitude, 'Don't ask me to take any steps'. Presently, however, he dropped his aloofness and we spoke more freely. When I mentioned the book I was planning to write on the Church of England he offered to let me have any information I might need, and before I left he said and repeated that he hoped these matters would not end with my visit today. I am puzzled by the Archbishop of Canterbury, he is a holy man and learned, but he seems to think that in his position he must be very cautious, a feeling probably explained by what he said to me in connection with our movement,

'Reverend sir, we have to remember that many of our own fellow churchmen to whom we must be loyal do not agree with us on these matters'.

After this interview M. Portal returned to France. The

friendships and acquaintances he had made would enable
him to continue his work with increased zest. The shortness
of his stay in England prevented him from visiting any of the
English Catholic bishops. This omission may have increased
the violence of the opposition which M. Portal later en-
countered from this source. It was not, however, wholly his
fault, Father Huby [1] tells us that a mistake in the posting of
a letter prevented him from answering Cardinal Vaughan's
invitation for the 14th of August and that he left England
without having discussed his plans with any of the Catholic
hierarchy.

Before starting for England, M. Portal had sent to
Cardinal Rampolla some notes he had written on the Church
of England, to which he had appended a copy of Lord
Halifax's letter to him of which an important passage is
quoted above, pages 33-4. The Cardinal had answered by
asking M. Portal himself to come to Rome. He arrived on
11 September. In his first interview with the Cardinal he
explained how he first met Lord Halifax, the long talk they
had together, their correspondence and how from all this
had arisen the idea of working together towards a reconciliation of the English and Roman Churches. He also spoke of
his visit to England and of the conversations he had had with
the various bishops; without attempting to minimize the
very great differences, he stressed the importance of the
catholic movement in the Church of England with which
he had personal contact and his view that this necessarily
involved a turning towards Rome.

The Cardinal seemed very interested and said to M.
Portal that clearly there was something here to be done, but
exactly what, they were seeking to discover. This last remark
surprised M. Portal, who had no idea that matters were
moving so fast. The interview ended with the Cardinal
promising M. Portal an audience with the Holy Father.
The following account of his audience with the Pope was
written by M. Portal immediately on its termination.

[1] 'Études', 5 March 1937: 'Lord Halifax', by J. Huby.

The next day, the 12th of September, I arrived in the papal antechamber at about twenty to six, and within five minutes was introduced into the presence of Leo XIII. The audience lasted about an hour.

'I sent for you to come to Rome,' the Pope began, 'and must thank you for coming so promptly. I want very much to talk to you about the English Church, but sit here so that we can talk in comfort.' I sat down and began. With scarcely any interruption I told him more or less what I had told Cardinal Rampolla the day before. The Pope followed me most attentively and it seemed to me that he had already been told in fairly long detail what I had said yesterday. His chief preoccupation seemed to be with the practical question of whether anything, and if so what, could be done. Since my interview the previous day I had been thinking a lot about this and ventured to suggest that a good method would be for the Pope to write a private letter to the two Archbishops. The Pope would say that, having already addressed the Eastern churches in inviting them to work for union, he now wished particularly to approach the English Church, but that before making any public approach he thought it best to write privately to the two Archbishops appealing to their love of Jesus Christ to work with him towards union. I explained later the importance of writing to the two Archbishops, not only to Canterbury, as we may expect great support from his Grace of York. I also suggested that a letter contain a veiled threat, in the case of refusal, to appeal to the Whole Church, as I felt sure that neither Archbishop would be willing to face the consequences of refusal, either before their own church or at the bar of history. Leo XIII's bright eyes lit up his whole face; he reflected for some moments and then said decidedly, 'Yes I will write that letter'; I was very greatly moved, as I had not expected such an immediate decision.

'But', said the Pope, 'let us consider the difficulties, there must be difficulties in the way.'

'Yes, your Holiness, there are great difficulties, one a doctrinal one which affects you yourself!'

'You mean my infallibility?' asked the Pope.

'Yes, your Holiness, but I think the infallibility could be explained in a way which might be acceptable to the English if one insisted on the means which the Pope must employ to ascertain the truth.' And I recalled my conversation with the Bishop of Peterborough.

'But certainly', said Leo XIII, 'the Pope must take means to ascertain the truth.'

'Unfortunately,' I said, 'there are exaggerations which do us great harm.'

The Pope then asked me about English Orders, to which I replied that I thought their validity was doubtful.

'But do you really think that they intended to do what the Church does?'

'Very possibly,' I replied.

'But would the political difficulties not be very great? To begin with the dependence of the Bishops on the civil power.' I explained that this dependence was not as great as had been thought, and cited the case of the Bishop of Lincoln who recognized only the jurisdiction of the Primate, the Archbishop of Canterbury, and refused to appear before the Privy Council. In speaking of my pamphlet I explained that our purpose in raising the question of orders was to create a point of contract which would give an opportunity to the representatives of the two Churches to discuss, in the spirit of charity, the differences which separated them. After some discussion on where such a meeting might be held, the Pope asked me to stay in Rome for a few days more and to come to see Cardinal Rampolla the next day as he would have given him his instructions. He then added,

'Oh, if only union with the Anglicans were possible.'

'By God's grace, Holy Father,' I said, 'it is.' And I repeated what the Archbishop of York had said to me, 'Let us hope that we are assisting in the beginning of great things. Your Holiness will see these great things.'

'God grant it,' said the Pope, 'I would then gladly sing my *Nunc Dimittis*. When I first spoke of union with the Greek Church here in this very room I was told I was speaking of a Utopia. I don't believe it because I think that in the midst of all today's impiety and revolution, people with no leanings towards religion will turn to the Church and that my call for union will not go unheard. I definitely do not regard it as a Utopia.' The Pope had spoken with great vigour ; he was truly magnificent. After a few moments the Pope asked after the Bishop of Cahors, and also after my Superior General M. Fiat. I then got to my knees and having blessed me and while I was genuflecting the Pope added quite simply, 'Goodbye Portal, goodbye.'

As soon as I got back, still much moved, I wrote this account of an audience which I shall ever remember.

Events were moving fast : only a few months had elapsed since the publication of the pamphlet on Anglican orders, and a double result appeared to be almost imminent. After three centuries of separation, there were to be revived direct communications between Rome and Canterbury, and the Holy Father agreed in principle to the doctrinal points separating the two Churches being studied by a mixed commission. The day following his audience with the Pope, M. Portal was again received by Cardinal Rampolla, to whom he gave an account of what had passed between himself and the Pope and of the suggestions which he had ventured to make. The Cardinal thought that such a letter might well be written, as it would be a fatherly gesture which could only bring honour to the Holy See.

Two days later (15 September), Leo XIII had changed his mind. He informed M. Portal through Cardinal Rampolla that the way was not sufficiently prepared, that a rebuff would be humiliating, and that it was better to take other steps. Cardinal Rampolla would write a letter to M. Portal which could be shown to Lord Halifax and possibly even published later. M. Portal observed that such an indirect approach, though it might appear more prudent, was far less likely to produce any result. The Archbishops could not possibly avoid answering a direct invitation, but to a letter not even addressed to either of them they, and especially the Archbishop of Canterbury, might well say there was nothing to answer. But M. Portal had already given forceful expression to his views and appreciated that the matter had been decided.

In view of the importance of this first attempt to make contact between the Church of Rome and the Church of

England we print in full the letter from Cardinal Rampolla to M. Portal, which was intended to be seen by the heads of the Church of England.

Reverend Sir, it was most kind of you to think of offering me the small work on Anglican orders recently published under the pseudonym Dalbus, and the value of this gift is greatly increased by the addition of the interesting accounts of the theological work and outlook of some of the most distinguished members of the Church of England who, as you truly say, in their desire for union await with anxious impatience the day which will unite, as brothers in one communion, all who truly believe in the redemption of the world by our Lord Jesus Christ.

I am happy to be able to inform you that, in spite of the many calls on my time, I have been able to read this work, which is being widely discussed, and have done so with great interest. I was delighted to find so intricate a subject examined with such complete impartiality and in the spirit solely directed to the search for truth in the spirit of charity. Dalbus thinks that the intellectual movement which started in Oxford and which is spreading in the Church of England among many men learned in the history of Christian origins and honest searchers after the truth, will finally result in dispelling ancient prejudices and thereby bring back into unity with the visible church of Christ the daughter of Rome, and that noble English race which received its Christianity from Gregory the Great. Thus the English will become fully deserving of the great destiny to which they have been called by providence.

No doubt whatever can be raised as to the affectionate reception that this nation would receive from its ancient mother and mistress if this happy return were accomplished, for nothing could equal the ardour with which the Sovereign Pontiff, who today governs the Church of God, wishes to re-establish peace and unity in the Great Christian family, and to reunite, as in one sheaf, all the forces of Christianity, in order that they may offer effective opposition to the torrent of impiety and corruption which overflows from all sides today. Certainly his Holiness will spare neither labour, nor care, nor effort to smooth the road, to bring light where that should prove necessary, and to strengthen the wills of those who, loving the good that they know, do not feel themselves as yet prepared to embrace it.

A friendly exchange of ideas and a more careful and profound study of former beliefs and practices of worship would be the most useful means possible to prepare the way for his desired union. All this ought to be accomplished without any touch of bitterness and recrimination, or preoccupation with worldly interest, in an atmosphere wherein one would breathe the spirit of humility and Christian charity alone, with a sincere desire for peace, and ardent devotion to the immortal love of God, who prayed that all His own should be one in Him, and did not hesitate to cement this union with His Blood.

May the members of the Anglican Communion have the conviction, living and profound as it should be, that the unity of the Church is the express will of Jesus Christ; that the divisions and various forms of religious beliefs are the cause of a state of things repugnant to reason and displeasing to God; that those who help to maintain such a state of things render themselves guilty before God and before society for depriving it of the greatest boon: *then* the hope of the return of England to the one centre of unity will not be in vain. As Bossuet says, so intelligent a nation will not long remain in such bewilderment. Her respect for the teaching of the fathers and her careful historical researches will bring her back to the teaching of the early centuries. I cannot believe that the hatred of the See of Peter from whom she received her Christianity will continue. May God grant that this great man's words prove prophetic, and one might add now, after two centuries, that citizens of a free country, the English cannot but desire that the reign of justice, order and peace should be re-established throughout the world, and that is exactly the most ardent wish of the Sovereign Pontiff Leo XIII. May this wish, received with fervour and seconded in sincerity, point the dawn of a great religious renaissance, of which modern society is so greatly in need, and put the English nation at the head of the salutary return of the world to the Christian life.

This letter, which reached M. Portal on 21 September, constituted a step, albeit a small one, by Rome, and an indication of a friendly disposition. It remained necessary to obtain something analogous from the Archbishop of Canterbury, which would open the way for a more formal approach by Leo XIII in the form of direct communication with the English Archbishops. M. Portal thought that there his work would be ended and that he would be free to restart his lectures at the seminary at Cahors. His only fear was that he might lose his position there; in a week he would have to be back for an October retreat, so he decided to go at once to England, and discuss with Lord Halifax how to bring about this result.

I had written several letters to Lord Halifax from Rome, but had not posted them as the Italian service is very unreliable, and such partial news as they had, made my friends even more impatient to learn exactly what had happened. I was equally impatient to tell them, and gave a most detailed account. We were all overcome, the results were so unexpected and opened up such vast vistas. I do not know how long I spoke, or for how long our meeting lasted. Night had fallen, and we were still together when a magnificent fireball flashed across the sky. Amidst our exclamations Lord Halifax said: 'It is the Star of Leo XIII.' It is known that a star figures in Leo XIII's arms.

M. Portal and Lord Halifax were, for a moment, uncertain of what practical steps to take. They would have preferred to approach the Archbishop of York first, as he was more in sympathy with their movement; however, out of respect for Primate of All England, they decided to go at once to Canterbury.

We left Hinkleton at ten o'clock at night arriving at the Archbishop's at nine in the morning. After some tea we were received and with the Archbishop was Canon Mason the well-known theologian. The Archbishop adopted a more reserved attitude than ever. I told him of how I had been summoned to Rome, and in great detail of the audiences I'd had with Cardinal Rampolla and with His Holiness. I explained how what I said was most favourably received, and of how the direct approach which I had suggested had been accepted and then changed, and what I considered the reasons for the change.

There were probably three principal reasons which influenced the Archbishop of Canterbury in declining to take the steps in the matter proposed to him by Lord Halifax and M. Portal. In the first place he was taken by surprise, and felt that he had been unduly rushed. There certainly was a letter from Cardinal Rampolla to M. Portal, but the Cardinal was not the Pope, and there would be an obvious absence of parity if the chief Bishop of the Anglican Church were to write as such in answer to a private letter from Rome. Secondly the Archbishop felt the need for caution from the fact that in the Church of England three different lines of thought exist : the Anglo-Catholics with a definite dogmatic faith and practice, fairly like that of Roman Catholics : on the other extreme the low Church, Protestants who reject many catholic dogmas, particularly that of authority in doctrinal matters. And between the two, the broad Church, who see no objection to the civil authority interfering in ecclesiastical matters, and whose doctrinal position is difficult to express in any definite creed or statement. The third reason which influenced the Archbishop was the Roman Prelates' striking lack of agreement as to their behaviour towards Anglicans, or as to the objects towards which they were striving. Cardinal Rampolla conveyed his esteem to Lord Halifax, while Cardinal Vaughan, in a letter to the Cardinal-Archbishop of Toledo, published in *The Times*, called him the 'Head of a Sect' and insinuated that he was 'subtly deceiving his Spanish correspondents'. Whereas Cardinal Rampolla was envisaging a friendly reconciliation, a reunion after discussion and equitable concessions, Cardinal Vaughan in a recent speech at Preston emphasized that only unconditional submission could be accepted, and this speech had never been repudiated by Rome. M. Portal's account of the interview continues :

I explained the purpose of the indirect approach was to give the Church of England authorities an opportunity to shew their friendly disposition by themselves making a similar indirect approach, and I added that as an earnest of his friendly disposition

Leo XIII was about to commission the Abbé Duchesne, to write a work on Anglican orders.

'But what steps should I take?' asked the Archbishop. I answered suggesting that he write to Lord Halifax a letter similar to that from Cardinal Rampolla to myself. The interview then became very painful. 'Cardinal Rampolla, said the Archbishop, 'is not the Pope. If the Pope had himself written the letter, then I could write to Lord Halifax. But it is a Cardinal who wrote, and if I were to write there would be no similarity in the position.' Lord Halifax and I tried to explain that Cardinal Rampolla was a Minister of the Pope and that from a governmental standpoint they were one and the same. It caused me real sorrow to see the Archbishop thus quibbling on questions of words and forms instead of realising that here was a unique chance of restoring relations with Rome and thrilled at the prospect of a possible union, I could not help comparing him, to his disadvantage, with Leo XIII. We left feeling somewhat aggrieved. The Archbishop had began by saying that he would not write this letter, but towards the end he seemed less definite. Lord Halifax, Canon Mason and I went for a short walk. I said to the Canon, quietly but quite clearly, what I had hinted at to the Archbishop, that the matter was in their hands, and that it depended on them whether any attempt was made to bring about reunion. History would judge severely those who repelled Leo XIII's advances, and it would have to be made known to the English public, that contrary to what is commonly said, it is not Rome which is the cause of the separation. I added without hesitation that, when all was said and done, I knew of a Greek Church and a Latin Church, a Church of the East and of the West, but that I knew of no English Church, and that for the Pope to offer to enter into negotiations with the Archbishop of Canterbury on terms of equality, which even on Anglican principles he was in no way bound to do, was very condescending on his part. The good Canon tried to calm me down, assuring that the Archbishop was a very good Christian and would certainly do all he could to promote reunion. What I never understood was that the Archbishop of Canterbury, after these centuries of separation should not seize the unhoped for chance of negotiating directly with the Pope who had made the first advance.

It was against this failure that Lord Halifax and M. Portal continued to strive during the last months of the year 1894. The Archbishop could not decide to write the explicit letter for which they asked, though he did on 15 October write to Lord Halifax : 'I need not assure you that I can conceive of no greater privilege or happiness than to be used by Our Lord as an instrument in reaching that unity which he treats as a consummation of his Gospel'.[1] But reservations followed immediately which diminished the value of this declaration. However, M. Portal thought that in the light of this letter Rome might well make a direct approach. The Archbishop would be obliged to answer, as it would be impossible for him officially to repell a friendly advance. Leo XIII on his side did not forget England. He made up his mind to write to the Archbishop, and at one moment he had been ready, as an earnest of his friendly dispositions, to provide that Anglican priests converted to Catholicism should be ordained conditionally.[2] But on the advice of Cardinal Vaughan he soon changed his mind.

Those favourably disposed to union were held back by well-understood considerations. Lord Halifax wrote to M. Portal on 5 February 1895 :

> The real difficulty lies in fear of public opinion. Our Bishops find it almost impossible to believe that any friendly overture can come from Rome. With yours, apart from the difficulties inherent in the present position of the Church of England, is fear of losing the advantages of their actual independent position, which might be affected if the Pope took some step which would irritate public opinion here.[3]

But anyhow Rome had made a gesture, and it was for the

---

[1] For full text of letter, see Appendix.—A. T. M.

[2] *Portal: My Diary*, p. 7, 19 January 1895.

[3] Compare Cardinal Wiseman : 'If one *must* err, if in mere tribute to humanity, one must needs make a false step, one's fall will be more easy when on the side of two theological virtues, than when on the cold, bare earth of human prudence. If I shall have been both too hopeful in my motives, and too charitable in my dealings, I will take my chance of smiles at my simplicity, both on earth and in heaven. Those of the latter, at least, are never scornful.' Letter to Lord Shrewsbury, p. 21.

Anglicans to respond to it. Lord Halifax took the reunion
of the Churches as the subject of his speech at the Annual
Meeting of the English Church Union on 14 February 1895.
The object was to elicit, especially from the bishops, an expression of opinion in favour of reunion, and to pave the
way for such conferences as he and M. Portal had in
mind. It amply succeeded and many letters showed,[1] along
with a sincere desire for reunion, a wish that the question
of Orders should be first considered. Armed with these
letters, Lord Halifax left for Rome on 12 March. At his
audience with the Pope on 21 March Lord Halifax asked
him whether, in view of the sympathetic attitude of so many
bishops, he would not consider writing a letter to the Archbishops of Canterbury and York similar to the one discussed
with the Abbé Portal. This would mention, *inter alia*, the
possibility of a conference between theologians, part appointed by His Holiness (including the Abbé Duchesne) and
part by the Bench of the Church of England to consider the
question of Anglican Orders. As his letter to Cardinal Rampolla of 8 April 1895 clearly shows, Lord Halifax's idea was
that such a conference should be purely friendly, providing
a meeting-place for theologians on both sides, and an opportunity to discuss not only the question of Orders but also all
those separating the two Churches. It was not to be in any
way a judicial body, to pronounce on the validity of Orders
nor even to advise on that matter. This was, as is seen, M.
Portal's plan, and he was in Rome with his friend ready to
advise him. But once again the Pope was unwilling to make
a direct approach.

Especially was he opposed to proposing officially that the
question of Orders be re-opened. All agreed that unless there
were friendly intentions on both sides it was a pity to stir up the
controversy. Catholics feared that if she again raised the question
of the validity of Anglican Orders, Rome would seem to cast
doubts on the propriety of her centuries old practice; also that
the Anglicans only wanted the recognition of their Orders to

[1] See Halifax, *op. cit.* p. 187.—A. T. M.

strengthen their own position,[1] to stop individual conversions by being able to say that they, no less than Rome, had valid Christian Sacraments. Anglicans on their side dared not ask for an examination of validity of their Orders for fear of seeming themselves to entertain doubts, or else that Rome should refuse the historical investigation which was asked for on the ground that the question had already been decided.

Clearly if such fears were well-founded it would be best to do nothing, but Lord Halifax's visit to the Pope was by no means without result. It decided the Pope to write directly to the English people asking them to pray for union, and the newspapers on 20 April contained a letter addressed, 'Ad Anglos Regnum Christi in Fidei Unitate Quaerentes'. After reference to the frequent meetings he had had with English people, meetings which had made him appreciate their keen desire to seek peace and eternal salvation in the unity of the faith, Leo XIII recalled the happy days before the schism, the misfortunes of the sixteenth century and the ceaseless prayers which had since been offered to God for unity. He praised the English for their piety, their devotion to the Holy Scriptures, as well as for their great concern for social justice, and finally asked for their renewed prayers. 'How happy we would be if, having soon to render an account of our stewardship to the Chief Pastor, we could present to our Lord some fruits of that desire for union which, under his inspiration and example, we have always tried to bring about. Difficulties are no reasons for refusing to labour in so holy a cause; the issues are not to be judged from a human standpoint, it is in circumstances of difficulty that the action of God's providence shines forth with the greatest splendour.'

This letter of Leo XIII had a most sympathetic reception in England. The *Guardian*, the *Church Times* and *The Record*

---

[1] Compare Cardinal Wiseman, *op. cit.* p. 14. 'I know what some will say,—that all this interest is of an *interested* character; that they wish to take so much from us as may serve to give consistency to their own Church, but have no idea of advancing further, or aiming at reunion with us. This suspicion is, I conceive, unjust and ungrounded: it is based upon ignorance of the true character and feelings of these writers.'

(a Low Church paper) agreed in recognizing its supernatural inspiration, and it was regarded as an important document coming after a separation of three centuries. It is true that the letter was in some respects disappointing. The existence of the Church of England as such seemed to be ignored. There was no definite suggestion of discussions or promise of relaxation of disciplinary rules, but it was all the same a call to reunion, and to corporate reunion. 'The expression corporate reunion does not occur in the letter,' writes the Marist priest, Father Ragy, 'but to anyone who can read between the lines it occurs throughout. Unless corporate union be understood many of its passages would be meaningless.' This was a point of primary importance to Anglicans.

All this was in the nature of an overture. Before trying any more definite approach Leo XIII was anxious to sound the feelings of the English, their reaction, in the Press and elsewhere, to a public letter from one whose name formerly aroused hatred. Such, he thought, would be useful to him in deciding what further action to take. However, in spite of the friendly and sympathetic reactions to his letter he made no further move, *e.g.* in the way of arranging conferences of Catholic and Anglican theologians. He did, indeed, think of modifying certain practices, but abandoned the idea. But he did inform M. Portal through Cardinal Rampolla that the latter's work had his blessing and that he would 'See with pleasure M. Portal taking a more direct part in this work (21 June 1895)'.

His superiors then released M. Portal from his teaching of theology at Cahors and he settled in Paris in the Mother house of the Lazarists. One of the first things he did there was to start a Catholic Association for reunion with the Church of England, thus carrying out the wish expressed by the Holy Father in his letter at 'Ad Anglos'. Its objects were stated to be: 'To unite Catholics in persevering prayer for the reunion of the island of the Saints with their Mother and to direct the efforts of each one so that the spirit of truth and love may destroy the existing barriers to such reunion'. The

Association published a monthly bulletin designed for a wide public. A special feature was made of reporting interesting contemporary events in the religious world. Nearly every number contained long passages of speeches delivered at both Catholic and Anglican meetings, and there were articles describing the situation in the churches on the other side of the Channel. Above all it acted as a bond of union between the subscribers, for each number contained a suggested prayer for unity.

The Association adopted a perfectly definite view on the question which had long divided English Catholics, viz. should one concentrate solely on making individual converts or should one aim at corporate reunion of the two Churches. From his study of the facts of the situation, M. Portal was convinced that the first method would never bring England back to Catholicism. It is quite true that the actual numbers of Catholics in England had greatly increased since the beginning of the nineteenth century but this was largely due to immigration from Ireland and the general rate of increase of the population. The sensational conversions of Newman, Manning, and Ward had not been followed up to any large extent, and Anglicanism, though temporarily weakened by their loss, had nevertheless continued to develop. Also a good number whose conversions had attracted attention had later returned either to their first faith, or else lapsed into complete scepticism. The Church of England seemed to be daily growing in strength. Since the Oxford Movement, she had been undergoing a spiritual renaissance in which she was gradually claiming independence of secular authority and increasing her prestige among the faithful. In such a situation M. Portal definitely believed that corporate union was possible : it seemed to him that only so could Our Lord's prayer for his disciples be one day fulfilled.

M. Portal's hopes were not based solely on this faith since he thought, as had Doctor Pusey and the Newman of Tract 90, that there existed no significant doctrinal difference between the two Churches. He appreciated that the Thirty-

Nine Articles were often interpreted in a heterodox sense, but he thought that they were capable of a meaning conformable with Roman teaching and that many Anglicans so interpreted them. He therefore had great hopes regarding the Anglican Church as a church in the process of evolution. Reunion was not presently feasible but would come one day. It is hardly necessary to add that, though convinced that corporate union could alone achieve real union, M. Portal by no means deprecated individual conversions.

It was not long before Portal realized that useful as the monthly Bulletin was it was not adequate to his purpose : a more specifically theological and historical publication was needed. From this need sprang the *Revue Anglo-Romaine*, which was published weekly in a format of about fifty pages octavo. Each number contained one or two leading articles written by some of the most learned scholars of the day — Duchesne, Gasparri, Boudinhon — and on the Anglican side Lacey and Puller. There was also a news summary and a section of reprints of small works little-known and difficult to come by, such as Forbes' *Considerationes Modestae*.

The first number of the *Revue* appeared on 7 December 1895, and in the editorial M. Portal wrote on the present being an opportune moment for seeking union.

The causes of our disunion are too long past to arouse animosity on either side. Many good Christians either ignore them or know nothing about them. Anyhow we are all living in an age of toleration and liberty unknown to our ancestors. Clergy and laity alike feel the need for those who acknowledge Christ to unite against the common enemy of God. In Anglicanism today a wholly new attitude is adopted in regard to Papal prerogatives. There are among the Bishops, men of great learning and great devotion who do not want the Church to continue in a state of schism so contrary to God's will. Reunion will come one day : even if the new attempt should end as have the others, in failure, our work is nevertheless worthwhile. For too long Catholic controversialists have argued against opponents they have never met. We will have accomplished our work of preparation if we succeed in bringing the discussions into an atmosphere more polite and more realistic. We have at any rate shown our wish for reunion and indeed we have taken the first step thereto.

Leo XIII's Encyclical had brought the question of reunion into the forefront. On 30 August 1895, the Archbishop of Canterbury published a Pastoral letter on the subject, and on 9 September Cardinal Vaughan spoke on the matter at a meeting of the Catholic Truth Society at which he announced that a commission was about to meet in Rome to examine the question of the validity of Anglican Orders. Also the Archbishop of York in an important speech at Norwich exhorted his hearers both to pray and to work for reunion. Reunion was then very much in the air, but in M. Portal's view the time had come for action to take the place of talk, the movement was entering a new phase and Rome herself was going to study the validity of Anglican Orders. It was more than ever necessary for the theologians of both Churches to meet and discuss freely and frankly possible bases of future reunions.

In his speech at the meeting of the English Church Union in January 1896, Lord Halifax said:

The real question we have to ask ourselves about it is this: Do we really desire peace, are we striving, however remote it may seem, to bring peace about, and in this our day to prepare for it? . . . Do we consider half enough what we might do to promote peace, or are we so immersed in our own affairs, too attentive to our own concerns, so absorbed in our own point of view, so indifferent and indulgent to our own shortcomings, so exacting in regard to the faults and deficiencies of others — in a word, have we so little love for our Lord and for souls that we are quite content to go on each in his own way, and to leave all thought and hope of the reunion of Christendom to some future day, which may dawn in heaven, but is never likely or intended to be realised on earth? It is not so God would have us understand His gift of peace. It is not true that He means it for heaven and not for earth. He means peace for time as well as eternity. Shall we not try to further the accomplishment of His

will? . . . That Leo XIII most earnestly desires peace, that
he is prepared to take the boldest and most generous steps to
promote and secure peace, none can doubt; but he has already
long since passed the years which are usually allotted to men,
and humanly speaking his days can be but few, and if a response
is to be made to his appeal it must be made soon. Do we realize
how great the opportunity is? . . . Ought not the Bishops of the
English Church, forgetting all else but the miseries consequent
on our unhappy divisions, the loss of souls which is due to those
divisions, their own earnest longing to see Christendom once
more at one, and the opportunity of doing something great to
promote the interests of peace which has been offered to them —
ought they not themselves to address a letter to Leo XIII? Only
think, under present circumstances, what the effect of such a
letter would be, saying that they too, in common with him,
deplore with all their hearts the miserable divisions which rend
Christendom into hostile camps, and keep Christians apart;
that there is nothing they are not ready to do short of a sacrifice of truth to promote the reunion of Christendom, and that
they would thankfully respond to any invitation which might be
addressed to them to consider, with theologians named by the
Pope, the differences which separate England from the rest of
Western Christendom, in the hope that, with the blessing of God,
a way might be found to reconcile them, and by means of such
conferences to prepare the ground for an eventual peace. . . .
How can those differences be set at rest if those who are apart
refuse to meet in order to discuss them? You say it is too
glorious a dream — that it is impossible. Why is it a dream?
Why is it impossible? It is dreams that are realized. It is the
impossible which does occur. Everything that has happened of
late seems to have prepared the way for such a step. The discussion on the validity of English orders is but a preliminary.
Everything might be possible if we had but faith. . . . Let us
keep the ideal of a reunited Christendom before our eyes, and
let us not have the shame and confusion, the sting and reproach
of conscience to learn, when it is too late, that all these things
might have been in this our own day if our faithlessness had
not hindered God's gracious purposes, if we had had eyes to see,
and ears to hear, and souls so attuned to the guidings of God's

providence as to discern the time of our visitation. [The *Church Times*, 24 January 1896.]

M. Portal printed a French translation of this speech in the *Revue Anglo-Romaine*, following it with a letter from Cardinal Rampolla, who also referred to the possibilities of mixed conferences. His conclusion was 'a friendly exchange of ideas, in other words such conferences undertaken in the Christian spirit and on the ancient formulae of our beliefs will take place whenever the authorities of the English Church agree thereto'. In fact thirty years elapsed before such conferences were held at Malines.

*   *   *

M. Portal had not asked for, nor did he want, the commission which the Holy Father had summoned to meet in Rome on 24 March. From the first his sole purpose had been to create friendly relationships between the representatives of the two Churches, and this was his object in asking the Pope to write to the two Anglican Archbishops, and in wanting to see started mixed commissions. He did not want things rushed, or any snap judgment made. He well understood the great initial difficulties which any work for reunion must meet, and felt sure that things were only at the preparatory phase, when it was important for both sides to get to know each other, and appreciate the other's standpoint, rather than start on official discussions. It is true that, once official negotiations were begun, the question of orders would be one of, if not the first, to come up for official decision, but this had not yet arrived, as indeed was shown by the diplomatic shifts on both sides. During this preparatory period — which might last some time — the question of orders was attracting attention in both Churches, especially in England, and the Anglicans were willing to join in conferences to discuss the question. It was clearly unfortunate to precipitate a definite decision on the validity of Anglican Orders by submitting the case to the Holy Office. Time and preparation were needed for the theological and historical works of Anglican scholars to become known to, and digested by, this supreme tribunal, and to lead those in authority to realize that it might be necessary to reconsider ancient decisions instead of just relying on a previous judgment. Above all time was needed to enable the more friendly atmosphere to spread its influence.

Possibly a good number of Anglicans did not appreciate the wisdom of these views. It is certain that a large number, over-confident of the strength of their arguments, were glad that there was to be an immediate examination of the validity of their Orders.

It was not, however, on these grounds that pressure was put on the Pope. M. Portal's activities and the interest they had aroused caused considerable suspicion in certain quarters. Many English Catholics, including Cardinal Vaughan, regarded them, first with impatience, later 'with "unconcealed dislike"'.[1] They thought that they would check the number of individual conversions: indeed, some said that this was their sole purpose, and that the question of orders had been chosen so as to arouse hesitations in the minds of those considering conversion to Catholicism. It is hardly necessary to say that M. Portal could never have been guilty of such disloyalty. Anyhow, in his view, the question of orders was somewhat far removed from that of individual conversion. People do not usually embrace Catholicism because of any doubts as to the reality of the sacraments of their own Church: such doubts, if they arise, come later, and the reasons for conversion are quite different. Indeed, it sometimes happens that the duty of believing that the sacraments which he has been in the habit of receiving are invalid, causes real difficulty in the mind of the would-be convert — a difficulty which would disappear if they were declared valid. M. Portal well knew — as the event proved — that an official condemnation of Anglican Orders would have no effect on individual conversions.

Leo XIII was, however, pressed to act himself, on the

[1] See Snead-Cox, *Life of Cardinal Vaughan*, vol. ii, p. 142.

ground that as the question had been raised and the theologians differed among themselves, a definite decision was necessary. So, though long opposed to the idea, he decided to appoint a commission of enquiry. It was charged to examine the question of Anglican Orders from three aspects: the historical, the theological, and the legal. The papers written by the members, together with a full account of the meetings at which they were discussed, were later to be sent to the Holy Office, who would examine the question afresh, and finally submit a report to the Pope, on which he would issue his decision.

The commission, under the chairmanship of Cardinal Mazzella, comprised eight members : the Rev. Dom Aidan Gasquet, Canon Moyes, Father David Fleming, Father de Llevaneras (a learned Capucin), Father de Augustinis (professor at the Gregorian University), Mgr. Gasparri (professor at the Catholic Institute of Paris), the Abbé Duchesne, and Father Scannell. The first three were definitely against the validity of Anglican Orders, the last four thought them at least doubtful ; Father Llevaneras's views were unknown. Merry del Val [1] was the secretary.

M. Portal was glad to learn that this commission had been appointed : he tried to regard it as some evidence of interest in reunion. It must, however, be remembered that he had hoped to get 'conferences on all questions in issue', not merely that of orders. The commission which Leo XIII had appointed was composed exclusively of Catholics, and so failed completely to fulfil M. Portal's hopes. The idea came to him that he might, so to speak, 'gate crash' some Anglicans into it.

The two Anglican theologians, the Rev. T. A. Lacey and Father Puller, S.S.J.E., could come to Rome, with the consent of their superiors, but without any express mandate, and be available to give any required information to the members of the commission. It might also be possible to

---

[1] Then aged 31 years. He later (1903) became a Cardinal, and Secretary of State to Pius X.—A. T. M.

continue stirring up public opinion in favour of such mixed conferences, for which a new occasion might possibly arise soon. In view of the problems to which the existence of the Pope's commission might give rise, another approach seemed desirable, and the presence in Rome of two Anglican scholars might facilitate the holding of meetings of quite another kind. It was important to seize the exact psychological moment for this, and a whole campaign was necessary, conducted on parallel lines with the Pope's commission.

It was to conduct such a campaign that M. Portal left for Rome on 31 March. It was of first importance to make known, in Rome, the extent to which the English Church desired reunion, and, for that, to obtain from England expressions of interest and sympathy which Rome could not ignore. To this end the Archbishop of York wrote to M. Portal on 27 March 1896:

I have for long been intending to express to you in writing what I have already said to you verbally, my admiration of your noble work in the cause of the reunion of Christendom, and the gratitude we all owe you. The publication of the *Revue Anglo-Romaine* which you started is a good occasion for me to convey to you my grateful thanks, which I do from the bottom of my heart. I find the Revue extremely interesting, and I much hope that it will do good by dispelling the misunderstandings, on both sides, between those who, though outwardly separated, are one in the faith of our Lord Jesus Christ. . . . We would welcome any opportunities of 'friendly Conferences' which might lead to bringing about a better understanding between us on the basis of St. Augustine's rule *'in necessariis unitas, in dubiis libertas, in omnibus caritas'*. I can assure you that Leo XIII's recent remarks on the subject of reunion have been greatly appreciated in England. They evince a great heart and a passionate longing for the unity of the whole Christian family.

This letter, coming from so important a person as the Archbishop of York, formed a most suitable counterpart to that of Cardinal Rampolla to M. Portal of September 1894 (see *supra*, p. 45).

The commission of enquiry sat from 24 March until 7 May, meeting three times a week. The meetings were private and nothing was to be said of what transpired at them. To this rule there was one exception, in that Cardinal Rampolla authorized Mgr. Gasparri to consult Mr. Lacey and Father Puller on any of the questions under discussion. As was inevitable every kind of rumour, on what would be the result of the enquiry, circulated in Rome, and the Holy Father's intentions became the subject of much speculation. The prevalent view was that the *status quo* would be maintained, and no definite decision given. This probably corresponded with the hopes of the majority of the Cardinals. Such a solution had the advantage that it in no way compromised the future, but fears were expressed that it would be liable to tendentious interpretations. Some said that the movement for union was the reason for wishing to avoid a definite condemnation of Anglican Orders, while others maintained that it was only the opposition of certain catholic circles which prevented Rome from correcting an earlier mistake.

Leo XIII seemed, personally, in favour of a cut-and-dried decision. He did not disguise his sympathetic feelings for the Anglicans, and he had been greatly impressed by the Archbishop of York's letter. Perhaps, as an earnest of his goodwill, he would go back to the practice of conditional ordination — of Anglican priests converted to Catholicism: possibly he would suggest mixed conferences.

These conjectures, which are to be found in M. Portal's letters and diaries, were more the result of wishful thinking than based on solid grounds. His remarkable optimism is reflected in his letters, as in that to Lord Halifax from Rome, dated 28 May, in which he writes:

I think the movement is about to enter a new phase, and widen its scope to an extent which none can foretell. The feelings in the highest circles here are excellent. But for these to be translated into deeds the Pope must find great support from your side. He must be in a position to reply to critics that he cannot repel your constantly expressed desire for reunion. This sums up our policy. I have no fresh news. The Abbé Duchesne is most hopeful, not of a formal judgment in favour of the validity of your orders, but of the final accomplishment of the work. There will be no adverse decision. The Pope has, before him, theological writings which will help him to lean towards reunion.

On Cardinal Rampolla's advice Puller and Lacey had remained in Rome so as to be able to visit the Cardinals; they were everywhere most cordially received. M. Portal writes to Lord Halifax on 16 May:

Yesterday Father Puller called on and had a long talk with the two Cardinals Vanutelli. He was delighted and most touched by his reception. When he left Cardinal Séraphino came with him to the door and kissed him goodbye. Both had told him 'You may be sure that nothing will be done against you'. That morning, when speaking of the Revue, Cardinal Séraphino had said to me 'We are really starting a new era'.

In England there was growing a hope that there would come about, if not early reunion, at least a positive advance towards concord. At the end of May Mr. Gladstone published a paper, entitled 'Soliloquium', giving his personal reflections on the subject. He noted how the recent religious renaissance in England had served to 'diminish the breadth of the separation between the Church of England and the authorized teaching of the unreformed Churches of both East and West . . . and so were valuable contributions to the cause of Christian reunion'. Leo XIII's initiative and his friendly gestures were signs of the times, and, added Mr. Gladstone, 'it is to the last degree improbable that a ruler of known wisdom would, at this time, put in motion the machinery of the Curia for the purpose of widening the breach which severs the Roman Catholic Church from a communion which, though small in comparison, yet is extended through the large and fast increasing range of the English-speaking races, and which represents, in the religious sphere, one of the most powerful nations of European

Christendom'. From the point of view of any future re-union, the results of an enquiry ending in the condemnation of Anglican Orders would be deplorable, and Mr. Gladstone wrote that he was convinced 'that if the investigations of the Curia did not lead to a favourable result, wisdom and charity would in any case arrest them at such a point as to prevent their becoming an occasion and a means of em-bittering religious controversy'.

M. Portal presented a copy of this paper to Cardinal Rampolla, who was much impressed by it. It showed that the interest taken in what was happening in Rome was not limited merely to the High Church coterie, but was widely spread. Cardinal Parocchi is reported to have said, 'Not since Henry VIII's day has there been such a movement towards union'.

All these hopes were suddenly shattered, and it was an irony of fate that what shattered them and put a stop to the movement which M. Portal had started, was an Encyclical on the unity of the Church. The interest in reunion then prevalent had moved Leo XIII to publish an Encyclical restating the traditional teaching of the Church.

A summary of this Encyclical (*Satis cognitum*), prefaced by a letter to *The Times* from Cardinal Vaughan, appeared in that paper's issue of 30 June 1896. It was from this summary that the English learned of its contents: the full text did not become available until some days later, after opinion on it had formed. Further, the passages appearing in the summary were such as to lead many readers to think that, in his anxiety to emphasize Peter's divinely given prerogatives, the Pope had given no proper place to the jurisdiction of bishops. Nor was this impression likely to be dispelled either by Cardinal Vaughan's letter or by *The Times* leading article, as the following extracts from the latter show:

The Encyclical practically deprives that controversy (validity of Anglican Orders) of all serious importance. . . . The terms on which alone reunion is declared to be possible are plain and simple. They are complete and unhesitating acceptance, not only of the primacy, but of the paramount and absolute pre-dominance of the Roman Pontiff over all professing to belong to the Christian Church, the entire submission of the heart and mind, the intelligence and conscience of Christendom to the decrees of the Papal See. . . . At any rate the Church of England long ago took a decided line on the issues presented very plainly in the Pope's Encyclical. . . . The claim of the Roman See to the succession of St. Peter is denied by the English Church, and the pretension that the visible Church of Christ is that of which the Pope is the acknowledged head is not less strongly repudiated. These declarations are to be renounced as pestilent errors before any individual member of the Anglican community can be recog-nized, on the terms laid down by Leo XIII, as belonging to the Christian Church. . . . The pretence can no longer be main-tained that reconciliation with the Church of Rome does not involve renunciation of the Church of England.

Thus summarized, the Encyclical produced the most un-fortunate results. All M. Portal's policy had been directed to trying gradually to persuade the English of the possibility of agreement on the subject of the Pope's prerogatives. This demanded great tact and infinite patience. He wished to begin by discussing less controversial subjects, and to pass on to the critical one only after the two sides knew and understood each other better. It seemed now that the very opposite was being done, and that every difficulty in the way of reunion underlined. Lord Halifax and his friends felt very deceived, and that this was a definite setback. M. Portal wrote to Lord Halifax:

Don't get discouraged. The *status quo* has not been altered, and the chief difficulty remains what it was, the Vatican Council. It is essential that you do not lose your tempers. All that you have said about the Pope is reassuring: you must continue to take the same line. I feel sure that the Encyclical will not have the un-fortunate results which you think. To dispel the effects produced by the manner of its presentation in your country, I suggest that you convene a meeting, which I will come and address, and you can publish what I shall say from the house-tops. I think that the surrounding circumstances will give a certain importance to my words.

The proposal was a bold one. It meant a complete change of policy, since in speaking on the subject matter of the Encyclical, M. Portal would be dealing with one of the most controversial and delicate of all the questions between Catholics and Anglicans. Also a London audience might still be feeling resentment at the Encyclical. Would it not do more harm than good? and would it not be wiser for him to retire and say nothing? But M. Portal did not think so. He arrived in London on 13 July, and on the following day addressed a gathering consisting mostly of English priests. He said: [1]

He who stands before you is a French priest, and a humble son of St. Vincent of Paul. You are prepared to give him your welcome and sympathy, not because you expect him to identify himself entirely with you in all your sentiments, or to speak to you altogether in the same terms as one of your own communion, but because you know that like you, and with you, he earnestly desires to further the great work of the union of the hearts of all who love our Lord Jesus Christ in one visible Church. Yes, I am a humble disciple of St. Vincent of Paul, whose name soars in a region above all human strife and all human divisions, that great apostle of charity both human and divine, who in modern times has done so much to heal so many sorrows and to soothe so many pains, and I like to hope that his children, animated by that same spirit of single-mindedness, humility, and love which it was his object to inculcate among his followers, may, by God's blessing, be instrumental in healing the wounds by which the Church, the suffering Bride of Christ, is afflicted. And I am also a priest of the Church of France — that Church so close to your shores which, as Cardinal Vaughan in a letter addressed to a French priest has lately reminded you, has in past days rendered some

[1] This version is the translation made by Lord Halifax and Father Puller, S.S.J.G., immediately after M. Portal had made the speech, and published in *Leo XIII and Anglican Orders*, pp. 332 *et seq.* It is slightly longer than in the French book, as it contains the whole speech.—A. T. M.

not unimportant services to your own Church — that Church of England which you love so well. And I am also a priest of the Holy Catholic and Roman Church, which is so dear to her own sons, and I am bound to that Church by all the cords of my inmost being, in regard to which you need no assurances from me that I would rather die than not believe as she believes, and not reject what she condemns. In particular I believe in the divine prerogatives of the Holy See and the successors of St. Peter. Nor could you yourselves for a moment doubt my belief, since were it otherwise I should be unworthy to be associated with you in that noble struggle which above all things demands the most perfect loyalty and truth, the struggle to win back for Christendom the reunion in one visible Church of all its members. It is now hardly more than a month ago since I had the happiness to say Mass at the tomb of the Apostles SS. Peter and Paul. Seven Sisters of Charity were also present, and close to them knelt two whom you know well — Father Puller and Mr. Lacey. I said Mass for the intention of the work of reunion. We all prayed for God's blessing on that great work, which, like all else that is really great in the sight of God, will be the result of those virtues of love and self-sacrifice so well symbolized by the religious habit of the daughters of St. Vincent of Paul. May it please God to realize the hope that the day may not be far distant when those dear friends who, to our and their great regret, are now unable to communicate with us at the same altar, may be enabled to be again completely one with us where they would most desire it. But if we are unhappily divided in certain ways, we are completely at one in a common resolution. We desire, with that energetic resolution which is stopped by no obstacle, we desire, I say, to bring our unhappy divisions to an end. Gentlemen, the reunion of Christendom is so beautiful a thing, that from the very beginning of our campaign we have been accused of seeking a Utopia which can never exist. This re-proach has been addressed to greater people than ourselves. When I had the honour of speaking for the first time to his Holi-ness about the reunion of the Churches, Leo XIII said to me, 'People have come to me in this very room where we are, and have told me that this reunion at which I am aiming is a Utopia'. We are then in good company, the company of the Pope himself.

Further, we are told that we are not only Utopian in our aims, but are also under a complete illusion as to the means by which these aims are to be accomplished, and that we do not see the obstacles which stand in our way. The fact is that those who speak in this way are themselves completely mistaken.

When Leo XIII did me the great honour of admitting me to an audience, he asked me what, in my opinion, were the obstacles to reunion. I replied: 'Holy Father, strictly speaking, there are but two obstacles — one, an obstacle having to do with doctrine, the other one relating to practice. The doctrinal one concerns yourself, Holy Father.' This I said smiling. 'The practical obstacles are ——' But, gentlemen, it is, perhaps, better not to name them here. Human passion, human feelings, and human rivalries are facts which cannot be ignored, and as to other difficulties which stand in the way they were foreseen, and those who are opposed to us know that we are doing our best to surmount them. Neither let them impute to us aims absurd in themselves, and which have never been ours. We have never desired a federal union of separate Churches. Neither have we desired merely an invisible union. We seek for the real, complete, and visible union which our Lord willed for His Church; we desire to promote the reunion of Christendom on the basis of one united Church, with its hierarchy, its government, and its faith. In reality these objections all proceed from one source. Those who make them do not believe that corporate reunion is a practical possibility. This is the exact point of divergence. The only solution of the question is in their view by means of individual conversion. I need not enter into the question why this view is adopted, but I can confidently retort upon its holders the imputation of entertaining illusions and aiming at Utopias. If people will face the facts, every one must surely see that England can never be brought back into Christian unity merely by individual conversions. No doubt the number of Catholics in England has largely increased, but to what is that increase chiefly due? To the Irish immigration. Moreover, the individual conversions which have already taken place have not produced the results which were expected from them. The conversion of Cardinal Newman and others, although it has deprived the Church of England of some of her most illustrious children, has not permanently weakened the Church of England. The progress of the great religious revival within the Church of England is stronger than ever. In presence, then, of the Church of England, intimately connected as it is with the national life on its political, its intellectual, and its social side, our position as Roman Catholics stands thus. The forces of the Catholic Church in England consist chiefly of Irishmen — a considerable majority of the clergy are Irish themselves. Is it probable, if we are to limit ourselves to individual conversions, that England will be won back by such influences? No one can doubt the sympathies which have always existed between France and Ireland, and which assuredly are felt most deeply by me; but here you are in the presence of a question of race which really presents an insuperable obstacle to your desires. Further, the English Catholics themselves are not uninfluenced by certain tendencies — the result of their isolation and of their persecutions in times past — tendencies which hinder sympathetic relations with the National Church, and so deprive them of that influence on its members which they might otherwise possess.[1] On the other hand the English Church seems to be growing stronger every day. Her members find in her services and sacraments and in the revival of the religious life the satisfaction of their spiritual wants; the conclusion of all which is that the method of individual conversions is not likely to produce any great effect on the mass of the population. For these reasons, and without forming any judgment as to the duties which might be binding upon individuals, corporate reunion would seem to be the method which ought to be preferred when we are considering the action of one Church upon another. And this not only because it is the only method likely to lead to any large practical

[1] Cf. Cardinal Manning, 'The long persecution of the Catholic Church by the laws of England has alienated the hearts of Catholics from the public and political life of England. Till fifty years ago they were legally *ex-lex*. The law is changed, but not the habit of mind formed by it. *Ecclesia patria nostra.* Catholics have not only been alienated from public life, but have been tempted to think that patriotism is hardly reconcilable with Catholic fidelity. . . . We have a million of people, priests, and faithful of Irish blood, faith, and civilization in England, and they are not only alienated from our laws and legislature, but would upset the ink-bottle over the Statute book. So long as this habit of mind lasts we shall never have a Civil priesthood; and so long as our priesthood is not Civil it will be confined to the Sacristy. . . . Many English Catholics, also, from religious prejudice are quite as incapable and useless.' From Autobiographical Notes written by Cardinal Manning in 1890, published in Purcell, *Life of Manning*, vol. ii, p. 774.

results, but also because it is most in harmony with our principles. Our fundamental principle is the principle of authority; moreover, this method of corporate reunion is more in conformity with the principle of authority, because it saves the individual from the torture of doubt, and other risks incurred by a personal investigation of the faith. You say to a soul which by its past, its education, and the graces it has received is bound by all the cords of its being to this or that Church — you say to such a soul, You are in error, and outside the true fold. Who does not see the suffering and doubt which is thus produced?

It is not, however, the suffering on which I wish to dwell. Who does not see the danger of such a shaking of the whole roots of the spiritual life? We hear much of conversions; but we are not told so much of those converts who have gone back to their original faith, or who have lost their faith altogether. One might name instances of men who were first Anglicans, then Catholics, and have finally ended in the most absolute scepticism. Such cases are the consequences of a method of proceeding which may be necessary, but which is often dangerous in itself. And this is the only method which, in the opinion of some people, is to be adopted for the restoration of unity. All souls are to be subjected to this torment of doubt and deadly disquietude. They have to ask themselves whether the graces they have received are real graces, or the illusions of the devil — whether the Holy Ghost has been acting on the soul, or whether the soul has merely been the plaything of its own imagination. And if it must be owned that these distresses have been the necessary lot of Anglicans in the nineteenth century, at least, if it be possible, let the Anglicans of the future be spared such torments. I plead again that it may not be deliberately insisted upon if another course is possible, and that members of the English Church may be spared all this anguish by the adoption of that other and better method, the method of corporate reunion. But is such a union possible? According to those who oppose our efforts it is not, and is merely put forward as a lure to prevent individual conversions; but, gentlemen, that is not my opinion. Corporate reunion is possible because it is necessary. Consider the present state of the Christian world. You are confronted by three great religious centres — Russia, England, and Rome. In Russia you are in the presence of a people which has remained more profoundly Christian than perhaps any other people in Europe. The power of Russia is increasing, not only by its conquest in the East, but by the spread of its influence in the West. What England is, you yourselves know well. I need not remind you what power and vitality marks its religion, or how great is the political influence which it exercises on the Continent, in India, and throughout its colonies. Rome, on the other hand, as in other things, so conspicuously in this, appeals to the minds of men by her wonderful organization and by her spirit of government; but Rome has lost the people of the North; she suffers from the loss of the Teutonic element, while among the Latin races, and even in France, which is more and more abandoning her traditional position of the defender of Catholic interests outside her own border, and chiefly in the East, the clergy, in spite of their apostolic zeal, their virtue, and their learning, in no way exercise the influence they ought to have on the affairs of the country. England and Russia then are the centres of religious influence of the greatest importance, and if, as thoughtful observers are beginning to think is not improbable, the Churches of England and Russia should be brought into a closer relationship than exists at present, it is impossible not to see that such a union cannot be without its effect on the Catholic Church and the Latin races. Union is necessary for us, if in view of the contingencies of such a future combination we are not to find our own action hampered. And union is also necessary for you. Have you nothing to gain in the greater strength such union would give you in your relations with the State, and in regard to your discipline? Do you not feel the need of having a centre and a head? Have we nothing to gain by union with you, by being brought into closer contact with your political and intellectual life? Our Lord has, indeed, promised that He will be with His Church to the end, and that the gates of hell shall not prevail against her, but He has not promised her prosperity, and her prosperity or the reverse depends on the exertions of her members. If we are united we are strong, if divided we are weak — weak and incapable of resisting the enemies of religion and society. Union, therefore, is possible, because it is necessary; let us unite, then; let us insist that union shall take place for the glory of our Lord Jesus Christ. And, gentlemen, I say again, such union is possible, and without compromise of principle. It is possible — nay, it is easy, in regard to all sacramental doctrine; for, as Dr. Pusey insisted, there are no irreconcilable differences between your formularies and the teaching of the Council of Trent. There remains the serious obstacle of the decrees of the Vatican Council; but, gentlemen, allow me to say neither is that an obstacle which is insurmountable. I will not, on an occasion like the present, enter into elaborate discussion; but I do say, apart from theology, when such men as the Abbé Duchesne and Father Puller think an understanding — an understanding, mark the word, not a *compromise* — might be arrived at, then such an understanding is and must be possible. Nor, gentlemen, is the Encyclical *Satis Cognitum* any fresh obstacle either. To say that it is meant to give a back-handed death-blow to the hopes of those who are endeavouring to promote corporate reunion is to attribute to Leo XIII something that is not worthy of him. I say that it is no obstacle if it is studied with calmness and patience.

The Encyclical lays down the oneness of the Church, and the means appointed by our Lord for preserving the Church in unity. It shows how the government of the Church depends on an Episcopate and a head, a constitution which enables the Church, always in subordination to the inherent rights of both powers, to centralize or decentralize her forces according to the needs of the times. After stating the prerogatives of Rome, the Pope points out that these are nothing new, not the result of a certain theory of development which would be inadmissible, but what was entrusted by our Lord to St. Peter and to His Apostles. The teaching of the Church today is not different from the teaching of the primitive Church from the beginning.

The prerogatives of the Pope are of Divine Right. Holy Scripture and the concensus of the early Fathers attest it. Surely the Anglican Church cannot refuse this meeting-point to which Leo XIII invites her? The Encyclical is very beautiful. It gives us the impression we experience when we penetrate into the essence of things. I repeat again — the constitution of the Church, as Leo XIII points out, is to be found in the powers of the Pope and of the Episcopate, and the rights of both have to be preserved. The constitution is Divine; but there is also the human element. It is Divine power, but Divine power entrusted to men. Hence it is that scandals have arisen, and do arise; but we confess our faults, and in confessing our faults we find the road to unity. Gentlemen, in conclusion, let me end by words of confidence. Those who oppose us, who declare that the idea of corporate reunion is an idle dream, imagine that we shall be discouraged by their opposition. They are much mistaken. We know indeed that there are obstacles, obstacles many and great, but we did not begin the work because we believed it to be easy of accomplishment, but because we believed it to be God's will; and we shall continue to strive on its behalf for the same, and for no other reason. Who would have thought two years ago that we should have seen the results which are already apparent?

In France, two years ago, we hardly knew you. Lutherans, Calvinists, Protestants of every description, and members of the Church of England, all were thought to be the same, and no distinction was made between them. It is not so now. In every part of France this question of reunion with you excites the keenest interest. You know what you are, and have been doing on your side on behalf of the same cause. To me, personally, it has been a source of the keenest interest to see what I have seen with my own eyes. That Mr. Gladstone should have spoken as he has is a fact of the greatest importance, and destined to bear much fruit. There is no one who has not been profoundly moved by the greatness of the ideas expressed by Mr. Gladstone and the touching humility, in all that regards himself, of him who says them. I would say to you all, Have confidence in Leo XIII. Despite all that has been said, despite all that has been done to hinder the accomplishment of his wishes, Leo XIII loves England. He said to me himself — and I may surely repeat it to you: 'Ah, if I could only see the beginning of what might lead to the reunion of the Church of England with the Catholic Church, with what joy should I sing my *Nunc Dimittis* — England in union with Rome would mean the conquest of the world to the faith of Christ'. 'England', as a cardinal said to me, 'has powerful friends at Rome.' When hearts are united the union of heads is not far distant. For the success of all works which relate to God, sacrifice is necessary. Who would not be ready to sacrifice himself, to give his life, if need be, to promote the great work of reunion? But God does not ask our life. He is content with less. He asks only our self-devotion. Let us give Him our heart, our wills, all the powers of our being to further this great work of reunion in the full confidence that He Who has inspired us to begin the work, will, in His own good time and His own way, enable, if not us, those who come after us, to bring it to its perfect and successful end.

According to all Press reports, this speech was enthusiastically applauded. It was of great importance, as the opponents of reunion did not believe that such a meeting could take place: even Lord Halifax had been doubtful of its wisdom.

No sooner was he back in Paris than M. Portal was summoned to the Archbishop's palace, when Cardinal Richard informed him of a letter he had received from Cardinal Perraud. According to this letter, written from Rome, the Pope reproved the *Revue Anglo-Romaine* for being 'too much under the influence of Lord Halifax and of the Anglicans'. Outside the Vatican there was talk of its being put on the Index. M. Portal answered simply that for him there was no question of obeying, but of knowing what he was required to do. In fact he was silent from that moment. On 18 July he handed over the management of the *Revue* to a small committee, and a few days later he was ordered to stop occupying himself with English affairs. Anyhow he was now tired out and about to leave Paris for a rest in the Pyrenees.

It is difficult to understand the Holy See's purpose in thus stopping M. Portal's activities. It is known that objection was taken to his speech of 14 July. On the basis of some very incomplete Press reports he was, quite falsely, accused of having failed to be explicit enough on the Papal prerogatives. He was also blamed for having spoken of reunion instead of submission: in this, indeed, the whole basis of his work was attacked. It seems, however, from correspondence passing between Cardinal Rampolla and Lord Halifax in August 1896, that it was as editor of the

Revue Anglo-Romaine that fault was found with M. Portal. At a time when questions about the English Church were being studied at the orders of the Holy Father 'it could not be pleasing to see that these same questions were being discussed by persons who neither had all the relevant documents before them, nor were of sufficient ability. The discussion often proceeded on a false basis, which was no help to the elucidation of the truth ; on the contrary a dangerous confusion arose. . . . The matters are so important that, to avoid error, the only safe course is to study the documents published by the Holy See. . . . The *Revue Anglo-Romaine* has not been condemned, nor will it be so long as those in charge are more careful and do not try to anticipate the decisions of the Holy Father.'

The decision was not long in coming. On 19 September the Bull *Apostolicae Curae* was published, which, by its declaration that Anglican Orders were absolutely null and void, put an end to all discussions between the two Churches. It came as a cruel blow to M. Portal who, in spite of all setbacks, had never given up hope. On the same day he writes to Lord Halifax :

Towards four o'clock yesterday afternoon the telegram received by the *Univers* was communicated to me. It is needless to tell you what MM. Courcelle, Levé, and I felt. Our first thought was for you and our friends in England — Puller, Lacey, etc. Poor friends, who have been so good, so generous, so loyal. There is nothing for it but to bow the head and keep silence. I talk to no one. Besides, the blow is so heavy and the grief so overwhelming that I am quite benumbed.

May our Lord have pity on us. May He at least grant us the consolation of seeing with our own eyes that we have not done more harm than good. You and yours have shown too much faith, too much abnegation, for your praiseworthy deeds and your sacrifices of every kind to be lost. They will help immensely in the salvation of your souls, and also (against all hope I hope) toward reunion. To you, my dear friend, I owe my highest joys — to work and suffer for the Church. I give you the best that my soul has of affection and unalterable devotion. I feel over again your great grief, and I suffer more for you than for myself.

Today's issue of the Revue contained no announcement. The next will reproduce the document, in a page which M. Levé and I have put together. That will be the end — the end of a beautiful dream. How it hurts.

Lord Halifax answered, on 21 September :

Your letter fills my eyes with tears; but it does me inexpressible good. Assuredly it was love of souls that moved us : we did not think of anything else. May something be done to put an end to the divisions among those who love our Lord Jesus Christ — those divisions that keep so many souls far away from Him — so that those who love each other, communicating at the same altars, may love each other more; in short, so that the essential unity of the Church of Jesus Christ may be recognized by everyone. To bring that about we must come together in a spirit of love and of charity, in a spirit also of penitence for all the faults committed on both sides; with a view to dispelling misunderstandings ; to distinguishing what is of faith and what is merely a matter of opinion ; to dispelling prejudice and, quite simply, to seeking the will of God, as He made it known to His Holy Apostles, and as it has been understood by the Church from the earliest times; and finally to establishing ourselves upon the grounds of Christian faith and practice required by the Encyclical (*Satis Cognitum*).

That, my friend, is all that we wanted. I suppose the others wanted it also. But in order to arrive at this much love is necessary, much charity, much patience, great self-denial, the wisdom that discriminates. Above all is needed that love-inspired spirit which, above all difficulties and in spite of all appearances, sees the essential truth as it actually is in itself, and neglects every personal consideration, trusting others as oneself, in order to make that truth prevail. . . . We tried to do something which, I believe, God inspired. We have failed, for the moment; but if God wills it, His desire will be accomplished, and if He allows us to be shattered, it may well be because He means to do it Himself. This is no dream. The thing is as certain as ever.

There are some bitter things which are worth all the joys of earth, and I prefer, many thousand times, to suffer with you in such a cause, than to triumph with the whole world. Your letter is more precious to me than I can possibly say. Troubles shared are already half assuaged; only I know that if we suffer, you are suffering still more, and it is this thought that hurts me most.

The Bull is of great theological interest. Leo XIII does not content himself merely with giving a decision : he proceeds to justify it, setting out the history of the former papal decisions on the subject. It thus appears that a previous judgment had been given on the 'Feria V' (17 April 1704) by the Holy Office, at a solemn session in the presence of the Pope [1] himself. One school at Rome regards judgments given at such a session as having special authority : it was on this ground that Leo XIII's decision was based. The Bull also explains that in the 1704 judgment, as well as in the fresh examination of the matter which had just been made, the only ground of invalidity relied upon was the insufficiency of the rite in the context of the intention of its compilers. That is, not its insufficiency *per se*, but relatively. Omissions which, in other circumstances, could have been disregarded (as not going to the root of the sacrament) were seen, in their historical context as evidence of heretical ideas in the minds of their compilers, as to the very nature of the sacrament, *e.g.* the suppression of all reference to the priest's power to offer sacrifice. Some Anglicans, including Lord Halifax, thought that the basis of the decision was certain conclusions of historical fact, and that, therefore, if further research showed them to be wrong, or doubtful, the decision itself could be modified. This gave them some hope.[2]

But, as M. Portal had foreseen, all work for reunion had to cease—for the time being at least. Neither friendly discussions nor mixed conferences were possible. Soon (November 1896) the *Revue Anglo-Romaine* came to an end : its purpose had disappeared. Something, however, remained

[1] Clement XI. The case was that of John Clement Gordon.—A. T. M.
[2] See Reverend W. Carson (a R.C. priest) : *Reunion Essays*, pp. 251-258.

of the movement. Without doubt the two Churches found themselves, at the end of 1896, much nearer to each other than they had been three years earlier. Men had met and come to know each other, and different points of view had been explained and discussed. The effect of all this did not disappear overnight.

From the purely scholastic point of view there remained the many articles on history, theology and canon law which had appeared in the *Revue Anglo-Romaine*, and which formed a sound basis for any future work. But perhaps the most important of all was that his experiences drove M. Portal to clarify his ideas, fixing on those which were essential, and thus to become the pre-eminent apostle of unity. He was the first to venture on this difficult path, the dangers of which he fully recognized. He failed, certainly, but as a soldier fails, who falls leading his men into action, and whose sacrifice is one of the surest pledges of final victory.

No future workers in the cause of reunion of the Churches could prepare themselves better than by studying this period of M. Portal's life. To him it was granted, after twenty-five years of silence, to make profitable use of the experience he had earlier gained.

PART TWO

THE YEARS BETWEEN

CHAPTER 4

M. Portal, Professor and Principal of a Seminary

In August 1896, in the midst of his worries over what was taking place in Rome, M. Portal was sent to take a retreat for the Daughters of Charity. They numbered four hundred and fifty. He then went to stay with his doctor, Dr. Ferrand, for a few day's rest. His *Revue* having come to an end, M. Portal was again free for other work, and he was appointed to the vacant professorship of dogmatic theology at the seminary at Châlons-sur-Marne. Before leaving to take up the appointment he received a letter from the Nuncio which somewhat cheered him up. He communicated its contents to his friend on 1 October 1896.

I am directed by his Eminence, Cardinal Rampolla, the Secretary of State, to inform you that you have the Holy Father's permission to continue those friendly relations with the Anglicans, to which you have given special attention, seeking to attract them, more and more, to the doctrines of the Roman Church, while yourself adhering strictly to the latest pronouncements on the unity of the Church and on Anglican Orders. By following the above instructions of the Holy See, you will greatly help towards the conversion of England, an object very dear to the heart of the Holy Father.

Leo XIII had wished to apply the brake to a movement which he thought was progressing too rapidly, without at the same time condemning an object very dear to him. The above reassured M. Portal, who now took up his new post, to which he devoted himself with his usual ardour.

At the beginning of the academic year 1896, the pupils at Châlons-sur-Marne learned that M. Portal was the new professor of dogmatic theology. He was not wholly unknown, as during the past months there had been vague talks in the college about the Anglo-Roman movement; also a novena of prayer for the reunion of the Churches had been held during Whitsuntide. His personal charm helped to create the feeling of friendly curiosity which soon surrounded him. He had such a new approach to both theological and practical problems, but, above all, those who came near him felt instinctively that great love of youth which always characterized M. Portal. To his surprise his new pupils took great interest in the Anglican question, the position of the Church of England, the desire for closer relations, and the hopes of those engaged on the problem. Still suffering from the disappointment of seeing the Anglo-Roman work ended by the new condemnation of Anglican Orders, and being busy preparing the last numbers of the *Revue* — in which its cessation was to be announced — Portal had not intended to explain the situation to his young students, and his first references to it slipped out, as it were, unintentionally. Those students of Châlons who were lucky enough to be in M. Portal's class enjoyed a most interesting year. They became as knowledgeable about the situation in England as if they had themselves been there. M. Portal seemed never to tire of the subject. He would speak feelingly of his first meetings with Lord Halifax in Madeira — in later life he often said that such a friendship more than made up for all the sorrows and disappointments which it brought. Listening to M. Portal his hearers got to know and love the loyalty, the generosity, and the piety of this great English nobleman, who believed in the real presence and the sacrifice of the Mass, which he attended daily, even in Catholic countries and who had once asked him why he was not given communion, as he believed in the eucharistic sacrifice as fully as any catholic. Others they got to know were the Reverend T. A. Lacey, a man of piety and learning very dear to M. Portal, and Father Puller, Superior of the Society of Saint John the Evangelist at Westminster, who, after a conversation with Mgr. Duchesne on the Vatican

Council, had said that he thought some reconciliation might be possible, which, as M. Portal would say, certainly seemed to show that something might be done.

So M. Portal's students learned that over in England were men of intense Christian piety, who had restored in their fullness the ecclesiastical and religious life. He would tell them of his visits to England, to parishes and religious communities, and especially of the welcome he received at the Society of the Sisters of Bethany, where the Mother Superior had just insisted on his giving a talk to the Anglican sisters.

It was thrilling to hear him explain how the Oxford Movement — a movement wholly internal to the Church of England — had gradually rid her of the Protestant leaven, and restored the ancient traditions which had never been completely lost but had merged with Protestant elements. Such a merger is difficult for the logical Frenchman to understand, as it seems to him a combination of contradictions. The English, however — and herein has always lain their strength — follow instinct rather than logic. A few of the followers of the Oxford Movement had indeed gone over to Rome, but the greater number had remained loyal to the national Church, working to increase its catholic doctrines and life. At the same time they did not cease in their desire for the reunion of all Christians, and men like Lord Halifax, believing that Rome was, by Christ's will, the centre of the Church's unity, regarded themselves in duty bound to work for better understanding, which should pave the way for ultimate reunion with the Roman Church. Firmly convinced that their Church was a true branch of the universal Church, with valid orders and sacraments, they disapproved of individual conversions to Rome, and worked for corporate reunion. The absolute honesty of such men as Lacey, Puller, and Lord Halifax, was beyond question, and in later days the Abbé Morel would smile when people in France used to talk of the conversion of Lord Halifax.

In a very real sense M. Portal's work was in spiritual

succession to the Oxford Movement. His sole wish was that those on each side should, through friendly personal contacts, come to understand each other's points of view. He did not seek to arrive at definite decisions on particular issues, and the reason why that of Anglican Orders had been chosen was that it had seemed of sufficient general interest for friendly meetings and discussions. M. Portal continually stressed this purpose, which was so often misunderstood. Soon his pupils became familiar with all the details of the Anglican problem, as also with his English friends, though they had never met them. Long after M. Portal had left Châlons, the first question he would be asked on meeting a former pupil was, 'How is Lord Halifax? What are your English friends doing?'

M. Portal's close association with so important and contemporary a question gave a special significance to his teaching on the doctrine of the Church and the sacraments, the subjects of that year's course. What is the Church's authority over the matter of the sacraments? What are the precise requirements for their validity? M. Portal introduced his pupils to the different opinions which had been held, even among Catholic theologians : some taking a more liberal view as regards the matter of the rite in the light of historical tradition, others maintaining the essential invalidity of the English Orders because of lack of intention due to the definite Protestantism of the first Anglican bishops. M. Portal's personal view was that Anglican Orders were of doubtful validity, and he would have preferred that this view should remain open. He thought that such a doubt would influence those who desired certainty in the matter to make their submission to Rome.

M. Portal never ceased impressing on his pupils the absolute necessity of history as the basis of theological study. He continually illustrated his teaching from historical documents. A born enemy of *a priori* theorizing, he would draw his pupils' attention to the important up-to-date works recording observed phenomena. As he used to say, 'the most elegant theory must yield to any simple fact, once the latter has been fully established'. Although most careful not to express opinions on subjects he felt to be outside his knowledge, he realized that to serve the Church it was necessary to appreciate the modern trend of thought. Speaking once of a recent work which had excited some suspicion, he said, 'Read that: it is the text-book of the future'. He also encouraged his pupils to become fluent in the living languages, especially German and English, so that they might keep abreast of modern theology. In addition to England, on which he was an expert, he would draw attention to other countries, chiefly Russia, in which he was beginning to take special interest. The numbers of the *Revue Anglo-Romaine* of this period show that M. Portal was then seeking information in this direction. Tavernier in France, and Birkbeck in England, had revealed the Russian world to him. He would talk freely of that great country, whose religion was that of the middle ages, and which represented, as far as the Orient went, the chief religious influence. He felt little interest in the other parts of the Orthodox Church, but he had a life-long sympathy for Russia.

M. Portal's outlook was reflected in his views on the relationship between Church and State in the modern world. These were based, equally with his approach to the problem of reunion, on realism and sympathy. His own beliefs were firmly grounded — loyal obedience to authority in doctrine and discipline — but he realized that in practical life one must face, fairly and squarely, the fact that they are very largely not accepted. He always looked for points of agreement rather than of disagreement, and his friendliness and sympathy succeeded in bringing people together and overcoming prejudice. To seek, in the spirit of love, to understand one's opponents' views seemed to him a better method of apologetics than the clear-cut and somewhat offensive dogmatism of a Louis Veuillot. Not that M. Portal's sympathy was uncritical : he was a good judge of men, and of things, but he was always himself infinitely friendly and approachable, which accounts for the sympathy and affection he evoked from all with whom he came in contact. The same spirit informed his teaching. One day the talk turned on the question of military service of the clergy. He said, 'Gentlemen, at a time when France is sacrificing her life blood to raise an army, the clergy must not seem to be trying to shirk this heavy burden. The law might certainly be administered in a better spirit, but we must all bravely bear our share.' How right he was was amply proved in the First World War.

M. Portal stayed at Châlons for a year only, but he left behind him a lasting memory, and his old pupils, on meeting him again, enjoyed going over the good times they had had. M. Portal, too, kept a lasting affection for his 'champenois'. Years later he would recall the surprise he had felt at the interest with which his first remarks were received. He used to admit that, stunned as he was by his recent disappointment, he would sometimes arrive in the lecture hall without having prepared his lecture, and almost without thinking speak to his hearers of what was nearest his heart. The affectionate sympathy of his pupils was, as he later said, a great solace to him at this time.

M. Portal never forgot the country of Champagne. A few years later he came back for a visit, accompanied by the Abbé Calvet and the Abbé Morel. His friend M. Flament (the author of a very good translation of the Psalms) was the Principal. M. Portal had a great regard for this modest and distinguished scholar who, shortly afterwards, to his regret, went out to bury himself as a missionary in China. Portal's visit was a red letter day for his friends. The sanctuary of Our Lady of the Thorn Bush was visited, where the Abbé Morel wrote a short laudatory sentence in Russian in the visitors' book.

M. Portal again returned to the Champagne country in 1921, while on a visit to the front between Malines and Champagne with Lord Halifax. They arrived at the presbytery on a Saturday afternoon, and on the Sunday morning

Lord Halifax heard mass in the parish church. In the afternoon they paid a flying visit to the field of the battle of the
Marne, near Vitry-le-François, and on the Monday they
went round to Châlons, after a pilgrimage to the chapel of
the Thorn Bush. Finally, after a short stop at Épernay, they
motored back to Paris. M. Portal had wanted to visit all
his old friends.

In the year 1897 M. Portal was sent to Nice as principal
of the large seminary there. The following summary of his
work is given by his old pupil, the Abbé Giaume, in the
obituary notice he wrote for the Nice religious journal.

M. Portal came at the beginning of the academic year,
1897 : he had, however, spent a year earlier at the seminary
(1882–1883) as a teacher. The college then occupied a
large mansion at the top end of old Nice which had long
dark corridors, and which has now been taken over for
municipal offices.

M. Portal was then in his early forties. He was of
medium height, erect in his carriage, with his head bent
slightly forward as if lost in thought. His features were well
modelled, and a pair of bright eyes shone under a broad
forehead, surmounted by black hair. At first we found M.
Portal somewhat surprising, but were soon won to him by
his charm. He was so completely natural and unaffected,
and had such a nice sense of humour. And how we just
hung on his lips during his lectures, captivated by the feeling
of his utter sincerity and that he was admitting us into the
innermost recesses of his mind. To most of us M. Portal
explained the importance of the doctrine of the Church :
he regarded it as the very cornerstone of all theological
study. When he spoke of the principle of authority and of
the obedience due to ecclesiastical superiors, his voice shook
with emotion, presently to lapse into a silence no less eloquent.

But all his thoughts and hopes were centred on the almost
inexhaustible problem of the union of the Churches. The
great English nobleman Lord Halifax always dominated

the picture, and then M. Portal would tell us of his work for corporate union, and of his travels to England where he had met a large number of the English bishops, and had visited all the Anglican religious communities. A completely new world was opened up to us. None of our textbooks spoke of the great catholic revival in the English Church, and the actors in this revival became alive in M. Portal's stories about them. In a few months we were familiar with the Oxford Movement and the Tractarian campaign started by Keble, Pusey, and Newman. In our spare time the keenest of us would browse among old files of the *Revue Anglo-Romaine*, the periodical which M. Portal had started and directed. Others of us would re-read or make copies of learned articles on the questions in issue between Anglicans and Catholics. The work at the college was, therefore, very concentrated. The most intelligent of us benefited greatly from the Principal's teaching, as well as from the large library at our disposal. After M. Portal's first year we moved from our old house to a new one at Cimiez, and there he altered the position of the library from the top floor, as had been planned, to the ground floor, where it was literally thrown wide open to us. And what an intellectual feast it was to have access to polyglot bibles, learned commentaries, Patristic texts, as well as theological and historical dissertations. In retrospect we could appreciate the intellectual intoxication of the Renaissance, when the treasures of antiquity were first revealed.

The occasional visits of M. Portal's French or English friends was always an occasion for excitement. Whether it was Lord Halifax, a man whose piety we all admired, the Reverend T. A. Lacey, Father Puller, or the Frenchmen M. Senart (a member of the Institut and a well-known Asiatic scholar) or the Abbé Boudinhon (later Rector of Saint-Louis-des-Français), M. Portal would bring them into our common-room and lead them into having real discussions with us. Not only were we grateful to our Principal for broadening our outlook by bringing us into contact with such men, but we were very proud of him. Whatever the situation and whoever he was entertaining, he was always completely at ease, the equal of all, high or low. He was indeed our 'Superior'. Why then did M. Portal leave Nice, where he was on friendly terms with the Bishop, Mgr. Chapon, and beloved of his students? The following letter, which he wrote to Cardinal Rampolla on 17 June 1899, gives the answer.

Your Eminence,

In ten days' time our academic year ends, and before the vacation — a time of travel and outside preaching — begins, I would crave leave once more to draw your attention to the present position in England which I regard as so important to the Church, and in which you are so interested.

Lord Halifax had promised to repeat his last year's short visit to us, but unfortunately he could not leave England owing to the violent struggle on which he has been engaged during the past year. But I have seen Mr. Lacey, the Oxford D.D., now a vicar somewhere near Cambridge, who came to Rome at the time of the discussion on Anglican Orders.

Mr. Lacey is one of Lord Halifax's chief lieutenants, taking part in all the struggles, and recently has been arguing before the Archbishops of Canterbury and York, sitting as a sort of tribunal, in favour of the use of incense in churches. Mr. Lacey stayed here for a week, and I had long talks with him, trying to become thoroughly *au fait* with the state of opinion in England. I would humbly submit to your Eminence an account of the impression I formed, together with a short summary of the events.

It is clear that both our campaign for unity and the catholic movement in the Church of England are responsible for the agitation. An unexpected result of the condemnation of Anglican Orders was that it pushed their bishops and theologians into taking a much clearer stand on catholic principles, that they might better defend their own catholicity. This has resulted in a very distinct advance in their sacramental theology.

The Nonconformists and the Low Churchmen protested, accusing the archbishops and bishops of betraying the Church of England, and they judged the time opportune for launching a

vigorous attack on romanism, seeking the help of secular authority
to control the whole English Church. Hence the double attack
by Kensit and by William Harcourt.

Kensit, personally, is quite insignificant. He is a London
bookseller who, a few years ago, was convicted of selling porno-
graphic literature in the shape of a book on sacramental confession which he had himself written.[1] His only importance is that he
chose the right moment to stir up protestant passions after Lord
Halifax's campaign which followed the condemnation of Anglican
Orders and the publication of the two Archbishops' Reply. From
the beginning of our movement a protestant reaction had been
generally foreseen — which was one reason for the great reserve
shewn by the Archbishop of Canterbury — but nobody thought
it would go to such excesses. A contributory reason for this is
certainly the ill-considered enthusiasm of some ritualist priests,
who have indulged in servile imitation of come continental
practices, without consideration for the feelings of their com-
patriots. However that may be, Kensit and his friends have not
hesitated to resort to violence. They have brawled during the
services, and generally made such nuisances of themselves that
the archbishops had to intervene. Sir William Harcourt, on the
other hand, raised the question in Parliament in July last. Since
Gladstone's death he is leader of the Liberal party, and probably
wants to gain the support of the Protestant party. So he made
a most violent attack, not only on the High Church but on
the whole episcopate, accusing them especially of romanising,
whereas for the English catholics he was full of praise. It's
always the same : Protestants and Catholics unite to deliver a
broadside attack on the Church of England. The Tablet and
their friends provided further examples of this. On the question
of the sacraments and the ceremonies connected with them Lord
Halifax and his supporters at once appealed to the authority of
the Church. Both at public meetings and in Parliament they
strongly repudiated the right of the State to interfere, and stated
plainly that they would disobey any Act of Parliament which
touched on matters of faith or discipline. The struggle in Parliament ended on 10 May last, with the defeat of a proposed law to

[1] I have been unable to verify this statement. It is the fact that in August
1889 'Truth' wrote, accusing him of publishing gross obscenity, and no action
for libel seems to have been brought.—A. T. M.

suppress the ritualists. The civil authorities have left it to the archbishops to restore peace.

The Archbishops of Canterbury and York are continuing the hearing: they are probably waiting for Parliament to rise before giving their decision, which is expected to be very moderate, for fear of stirring up demand for state intervention. But it is certain that if the ritualists have to give up certain things, *e.g.* incense and possibly reservation of the Blessed Sacrament, the fundamental principles will be secured. Anyhow it is really important that the archbishops can hear and decide these cases, without state intervention.

In all this Lord Halifax has worked indefatigably. As well as courage he has shewn great political wisdom, and his position is more secure than ever. The English Church Union, of which he is President, has increased its membership: 6,000 new members since last September. I am also very glad to say that Lord Halifax's views as regards Rome have in no way changed. He still regards the see of Peter as the *terminus ad quem* of his efforts. I cannot believe that his work towards this is ended, but hope that he will again work towards reconciliation. My daily prayers are with this intention, and my own humble prayer is that the Almighty will allow me to devote my life to so fine a work. I am etc.

By this last sentence M. Portal intimated to Cardinal Rampolla his view that he could best serve the cause of reunion either in Paris or elsewhere where he could give it more undivided attention. Possibly the Cardinal intervened: in any case M. Portal was recalled to Paris by his superiors to take charge of a new foundation, the seminary of St. Vincent, a counterpart of the Sulpician college at Carmes.

CHAPTER 5

The Foundation of the Seminary of St. Vincent of Paul

M. PORTAL'S two years as Principal of the seminary at Nice did not stand out in his memory as did his time at Châlons. He seldom spoke of them and rarely met any of the old students. From afar he followed with interest the careers of those who had come under his influence and whose development he felt able to help. I was at Carmes while he was at Nice, and he encouraged me to devote myself to the *Revue d'Histoire et de Littérature Religieuse*, a first-class periodical which had not then become suspected of unorthodoxy. He thought very highly of the Abbé Lejay, its editor, who had an equal regard for M. Portal. He also encouraged me to get to know M. Levé, who had been a great help in the production of the *Revue Anglo-Romaine*.

But Nice was a long way from Paris and M. Portal was very pleased when, in the autumn of 1899, he was recalled and put in charge of the Seminary of St. Vincent of Paul which had just been opened at 88 rue du Cherche-Midi. There were then a large number of theological students at the Catholic Institute and the old house of Carmes was too small to hold them all. The Lazarists were asked to start and manage a second seminary for the Institute and for this work no one was better suited than M. Portal.

M. Calvet's *Life of the Abbé Morel*, which the author tells us was inspired by M. Portal, shows how the latter interpreted his task. He was able to put in operation the two complementary methods on which he always relied. The publication of a *Revue* and the organising of discussion groups.

As always, M. Portal attached importance to accurate factual information on the situation in the contemporary intellectual and religious life, Catholic and non-Catholic. So the young whom he guided were encouraged to read and to analyse such publications as would give accurate information of the life and affairs of a particular country, Church, or group, such as the *Church Times* or the *Guardian*.

In the discussion groups M. Portal was careful to bring together people of the most varied opinions, devout Catholics and Anglicans, Protestants and Unbelievers, or one would find grouped together, theologians, philosophers, economists, scientists, men of letters, academicians and business men. All enjoyed coming, being attracted by the sympathetic atmosphere which M. Portal created. Also one was always sure to hear matters of interest discussed, and of meeting people worth knowing.

M. Portal derived great pleasure from the groups and the resulting friendships and he carried on the work till the end of his life. Even when he had to give up directing the seminary, he was able to continue them in his own home. He had a real flair for getting people together and was delighted whenever he had thus advanced the common cause or given help or pleasure to his friends. Few rooms in Paris have seen so many people or heard such interesting conversations as M. Portal's. None where so many ideas were discussed or so much good done. 'If only these walls', he would say in his study in the rue de Grenelle, 'could tell what they had seen and heard.' His sheer personality had made his apostolate a most fruitful one, and few people have done so much to make Catholicism understood and admired: abroad as well as in France.

M. Portal's friends were numberless and increased with every year. In the lecture he gave at Louvain (characteristically entitled 'The Uses of Friendship in Church Union'), he mentions some of the oldest, *i.e.* Eugène Tavernier, the editor of the *Univers* and one of his collaborators on the *Revue Anglo-Romaine* ; Anatole Leroy-Beaulieu, the author of

The Empire of the Tzars, whom M. Portal held in great esteem ; and Henri Lorin, friend of Cardinal Rampolla, one of the first Christian socialists and founder of the weekly socials. The Russian philosopher Vladimir Soloviev had stayed with Lorin at his country house at Maule where he had written some of his work — *Russia and the Church Universal*. Lorin used to tell how Soloviev, after writing half the night, would come and read the result to him. Usually Lorin approved of it but sometimes he would say, with his usual brusqueness, that he didn't understand a word, when Soloviev would tear it up and begin all over again.

Henri Lorin kept open house and loved surrounding himself with all the interesting and eccentric people he could, among whom was a famous Monseigneur Benigni, who later conducted a veritable military operation against all who were rightly or wrongly suspected of modernism. Benigni had even borrowed money from Lorin. At the beginning of Pius X's pontificate, Lorin asked him what the new Pope was going to do, to which the Italian replied, miming very suggestively, 'Pius X will go into a corner and squeak, then into another corner, squeak again and so on '. Henri Lorin had not perhaps that broad outlook which one met in M. Portal's other friends, but Portal valued him greatly as a fine character and firm friend. He always had his place laid at M. Portal's table ; he came as he liked and often brought friends 'to see the world'. It was thus that Mr. Nepluyef, the great Russian philanthropist, came to know M. Portal.

Among the regular attendants at the Sunday gatherings were the students of the secondary teachers' training college. M. Portal was cut out for the part of Chaplain to the group of practising Catholic students, an entirely informal position which he held for a quarter of a century. His young friends enjoyed the complete intellectual freedom which obtained, and at the same time they appreciated M. Portal's unaffected and deep spirituality — a spirituality based on the school of St. Vincent and ever informed by his devotion to the Church.

He started regular divinity courses, but derived even greater satisfaction from the retreats he used to conduct for these young students, either at Saint-Germain or at Chantilly. M. Portal's great success in dealing with the youth of the university did not fail to excite some jealousy and many attempts were made to divert his work into other directions, but his young friends stood firmly by him, among whom was Bera, one of M. Portal's favourite followers, whose early death in the Great War was a great grief. M. Portal thought that by interesting the young who came to his meetings in the work he was doing, by opening their eyes to its immense possibilities, he was doing them a great service, and he also hoped to find, as he in fact did, helpers both in the work and in the literature he was planning. But he never imposed conditions on any help he gave and none could accuse him of seeking in any way to fetter their complete freedom or interfere with their own work. On the contrary he was always ready to help anyone, even those who had more or less forgotten or ignored him. M. Portal's ambition was, by mixing up both theological and secular students in his study groups at the St. Vincent's Seminary, to secure that each should get to understand the other's points of view, and become people able both to understand their times and to make themselves understood. Circumstances, however, prevented the complete success of his hopes. The students had to give time to preparing for their own examinations, and the narrow book teaching of the university hindered the development of M. Portal's ideas. This was probably why some of the best friends showed no more than sympathetic interest in his schemes. Only a small minority realized how truly creative was this new method, how true to real life and how in line with contemporary ideas ; here too M. Portal was a forerunner. At the time of the founding of the Catholic Institute's second seminary, all seemed favourable to a great intellectual and spiritual revival, covering all departments of catholic thought. Although fully alive to the importance of sociology, M. Portal did not feel called to its study. He had enough to do on the intellectual and religious side, but to encourage mutual study, a society was started with two sections, one philosophical, the other religious, the latter being M. Portal's province, but this did not last long. Modern philosophy raises intricate and controversial questions and after a few months of work together it was realized that the two sides had better work independently, so the group on Christian philosophy continued under Father Laberthonnière, that on religion remaining under M. Portal.

One can truly say of M. Portal that he was a Catholic in the best sense of that word. He suffered much on account both of his views and his activities, but he never for a moment contemplated any rebellion or failed in complete obedience to the orders of the Church both in matters of faith and conduct. Any advice he gave to others was actuated by the same spirit. He had been among the first to recognize the Abbé Loisy's great ability and had got him to write for the *Revue Anglo-Romaine*. He saw in him one of the first contemporary exegetes, but always maintained that it was Loisy's philosophy, not his exegesis, which had brought about his loss of faith, and indeed it is difficult to reconcile belief in a supernatural religion with the pantheistic metaphysic of Loisy's writings.

In M. Portal's view the pastoral ministry and its contacts with human souls was the best preventative against over-absorption in scientific or philosophical abstractions. 'Always do some pastoral work' was his advice to any devotees of scholarship. He himself always kept in touch with the Sisters of Reuilly, whom he visited every week, and he likewise kept his confessional at the Lazarist house. He gave himself too, heart and soul, to the work of Javel.

The study groups, interesting though they were, did not take up all M. Portal's time. He well understood the influence which can be exercised by a periodical, and his happy memories of the *Revue Anglo-Romaine* encouraged him in the hope of being able later to found its successor. Thus came into existence the *Petites Annales de Saint-Vincent-de-Paul*, which sought to serve a double purpose ; the first devotional, especially for the Daughters of Charity, the second seeking to recover the work of the earlier *Revue*. It was conceived on a less ambitious scale, but in the same spirit. In one sense its scope was enlarged, as M. Portal's contributions dealt with all aspects of the religious life throughout the whole world and not merely with England. The devotional and spiritual side of the *Petites Annales* were no less worth reading than the theological. M. Portal's spirituality was inspired by the teaching and spirit of St. Vincent, for whom he entertained a truly filial affection and whose personal qualities no less than his historical importance he loved to study. He saw in St. Vincent's character a mixture of subtlety and clear-sightedness, tempered by a common-sense which led him to apply pragmatic tests rather than *a priori* principles to the making of rules. This he regarded as typical of French piety. Above all he admired St. Vincent as a great reformer who had done so much to increase the educational standards, and thereby the prestige, of the French clergy. Connected with the cult of St. Vincent was the great purpose of M. Portal's life—Union—which he saw as the proper result of reform. The nearer separated Churches draw to the heart of Christ the closer they draw to one another. For this reason M. Portal would, as occasion offered, try to make known to the separated Churches the great French Catholic Renaissance of the seventeenth century.

The purpose of the *Petites Annales* was not only to describe St. Vincent's past work, but also to suggest new ways in which the apostleship of charity might become more fruitful. All through his life M. Portal retained his interest in St. Vincent and his work, and he would often discuss it with friends, especially those whose studies brought them in contact with that period of French history. One of his few writings was a short study dealing with the extant portraits of St. Vincent of which the one in the great seminary at Nancy struck him particularly for its youth and energy, in spite of a certain melancholy. He had engravings made of it in different sizes which he willingly gave away as presents. The closing lines of his article on St. Vincent are worth quoting.

All who are familiar with the history of the seventeenth century, particularly the movement of reform of the Catholic Church in France, know that in his eyes it was an absolutely essential work. As he wrote to one of his priests, 'What the Church needs above all are Evangelists, men who will labour to purge her, to enlighten her, and to unite her to her divine spouse.' It was of this work, which revitalized French religion and has largely influenced the whole Christian world, that St. Vincent of Paul was one of the chief architects.

Interesting as were the *Petites Annales* they were but a beginning, and M. Portal's dream was realized when in 1904 the *Revue des Églises* was produced. This was true to its title, for not only did the Church of England figure largely, but notice was also taken of the Eastern and of the Protestant Churches, and the progress of Catholicism, especially in France, was fully set out. The whole was presented as objectively as possible and pervaded by that spirit of real charity which was M. Portal's distinguishing characteristic. The *Revue* lasted for five active and happy years. The widespread reactionary movement which then developed brought it to an end, not without great heartache for the editor and his associates. 'We put in some good work', he would say, looking with pride at the five bound volumes standing next to the three of the *Revue Anglo-Romaine*. The disappearance of the *Revue* left a void felt both in France and abroad, where it had perhaps been even more highly valued, for it was through the *Revue* that the influence of the small group of the rue du Cherche-Midi became so widespread, extending into the innermost parts of Russia. Many, if not most, of the articles owed their origin to the meetings and discussions which took place there. The same reactionary storms struck both, but M. Portal retired from the scene with complete dignity, though he was disappointed with the little support he got. He left the seminary of St. Vincent of Paul without complaining, recalling the old Portuguese proverb of which he was so fond: 'Deus escreve direito per linhas tortas' ('God writes straight on crooked lines').

CHAPTER 6

The Apartment in the rue de Grenelle

[*Translator's Foreword to Chapter 6.* On leaving the Seminary of St. Vincent, M. Portal, with his Superiors' permission, rented the second and third floors of a house at No. 14 rue de Grenelle, where he started a small community of ten to twelve boarders. See *L'Amitié au service de l'union*, by the Abbé Gratieux, Paris, 1950, p. 153.]

M. PORTAL's friends soon learned the way to his new home. It was a great thing, anyhow, to have kept intact the centre of the work, and the new flat was an improvement on the one in the rue du Cherche-Midi. Apart from a rather dark entrance hall, the rooms were lighter and brighter. It was also well situated in the heart of Paris. M. Portal liked it, and it is in this setting that his friends like to remember him.

The eager ascent of the two flights of stairs always ended in such a kindly welcome, either from the Master himself, or from his maid, Miss Cecily. If one came in the morning, even though unexpectedly, an invitation to lunch followed — subject, nominally, to Miss Cecily's approval, but she was usually found to have anticipated it. Likewise the afternoon visitor was asked to tea, and M. Portal brewed an excellent pot : he had his own special tea, sent direct from China in beautifully painted boxes, which he used to say was second only to what came overland from Russia.

And over our cups of tea he would question one : 'What are you doing now ?' 'Are you engaged this evening ? or tomorrow ?' And so he would arrange one's time in Paris. 'You must not fail to call on so and so. Nothing much may come of it, but you must keep in touch.' 'There is this man you must see : use my name as an introduction.' But sometimes a lunch, a dinner, or an evening party at M. Portal's would be arranged. 'Keep yourself free for such an evening. Mr. X is coming, and you will be interested in meeting him.' An invitation from M. Portal was a coveted privilege, and was always accepted with alacrity. At other times he would take one to lunch or dine with his friends. In bringing people together M. Portal was unequalled, and two days in Paris in his company did more to extend one's knowledge of people and events than two weeks spent elsewhere.

Conversation was encouraged by the friendly atmosphere of the small study, almost monastic in its simplicity. On the left, going in, was a large bookcase full of many important works, especially those dealing with English affairs. On the right was the fireplace, over which hung a large mirror, which greatly increased the brightness of the room. A few chairs and a small table near the window comprised the furniture. On the mantlepiece stood a crucifix flanked by two Russian ikons, souvenirs of Morel, whose portrait also stood there. Opposite the table was the door leading to M. Portal's bedroom, even more austere in its furnishings.

It was in this setting that one held those rather jerky conversations which M. Portal loved so much; jumping from Paris to Rome, from England to Russia. Past memories were called up, and plans for the future discussed. Sometimes one touched even on politics, only to find that this priest, who never concerned himself with them, was as well, if not better, informed than anyone in Paris. M. Portal, too, had a large circle of friends and admirers : Messrs. Georges Goyau and Pinon of the *Revue des Deux Mondes,* and Étienne Lamy and Frédéric Masson of the Academy. And one of his greatest friends, very much taken into his confidence, was M. Senart, of the Institut, one of the leading authorities on the languages and literature of India, and a man of outstanding goodness.

Not only among the laity but in all ranks of the clergy M. Portal had numerous friends. Mgr. Boudinhon and Mgr. Duchesne, who had both taken part in the Anglo-Roman campaign and many others never came to Paris without visiting M. Portal. And apart from friends were the innumerable number of men and women, rich and poor, French and foreigners, who came to seek his advice or help. Hardly was one visitor leaving, before another was being announced. When M. Portal wanted to be quiet, he would take his visitor for a walk along the neighbouring boulevards. He enjoyed those walks, especially on fine days, and usually took them just after lunch or dinner. He was such a true Parisian that the noise and movement in the streets, so far from worrying him, acted as a mental stimulant.

But amidst all this activity there was something lacking. M. Portal had started the boarding-house — with all its financial commitments — hoping to gather round him a group of men (including perhaps foreigners) who, although each would have his personal interests and work, would be inspired with the desire to help forward the great cause of reunion. In such a hope he was destined to be disappointed, as no one seemed particularly interested in this work, and for years there continued to live under his roof professors preparing their lectures, students working for their examinations or writing their theses, who, when they met for meals, usually talked about the weather.

Nor was this M. Portal's only trial. He suffered as much as any from the contemporary anti-modernist reaction. All direct action or writing was forbidden him, and he used to wonder whether, as no periodical was possible, some book or pamphlet or serial publication could be arranged. Long inaction got him down, and one rarely met him without him broaching these matters. He was always urging his friends to write, whether for newspapers or periodicals. He also suffered greatly when he saw his friends suspected and frustrated in their work. Never, however, did he counsel anything other than submission and patience.

The work was still there to be done, and the important thing was to train workers for the future, when it could again be taken in hand. This was by no means easy. We all, especially when young, prefer a short-term job with a clear-cut objective. The Slav outlook, especially, seems rather to repel, by reason of its wide and somewhat imprecise range. A thesis on some obscure classical author of the past seems an easier work than the exploring of these wide uncharted seas. And yet a world exists there whose study is vitally necessary from all points of view — political, moral, and religious. We are very much the poorer for our lack of knowledge of Russia. M. Portal felt this strongly, and constantly directed the attention of his friends in this direction, though not with much success: neither clergy nor laity evinced any great vocations for work in the East. But M. Portal never gave up trying. He knew that one must knock at many doors before finally coming to the one which would open, and he never regretted his unsuccessful attempts. He had faith that, in God's overall plan and in His good time, all such would bear fruit.

Not that he was without sensitivity: on the contrary he suffered greatly from the disaffection and misunderstanding of his friends, and particularly when an old pupil took a diametrically opposite position on some fundamental question. One day, when a former fellow worker hinted that the time had come for him to retire from the scene, M. Portal replied, 'To whom do you say that? Perhaps it does not fall to you to remind me.'

There were, however, consolations. His young college friends remained unshakeably faithful; his great evangelical work at Javel was flourishing, and his influence was extending in many different fields. Also he had many friends and sympathizers among the intellectuals of the day, especially M. Paul Boyer, the Director of the School of Modern Oriental Languages. This friendship was fully reciprocated, and M. Portal sent many of his new recruits to M. Boyer's Russian lectures. In spite of everything there were real grounds for hope: plans were being prepared, and vocations fostered, often under great difficulties. M. Portal realized that his work was in preparation for a future time when it would be a matter of pride to say that one had lived through the present.

CHAPTER 7

M. Portal's Theology

IF bookishness and pedantry be the marks of a learned man, M. Portal was not one. He was certainly a good writer, as his few surviving works show. He was, however, a born enemy of that pomp, that oratorical over-emphasis which characterize so much religious writing. To him, what mattered was clear and exact exposition based on established facts. He was truly of the school of St. Vincent, linked to the best traditions of a great epoch and also at one with the modern scientific method which demands as precise a presentation of reality as possible.

He himself wrote, under the pseudonym Fernand Dalbus, a most interesting pamphlet on Anglican Orders. It can still be read with profit and interest, combining a sound theological basis with accurate historical knowledge. His judgments too are always most fair. It shows us what M. Portal might have accomplished in this field. It was not, however, his vocation. He was a man of action, not himself a theologian but a purveyor of material for theologians, suggesting subjects to be considered and points of view to be taken into account, and no one ever regretted following the advice he gave on these matters. As has been seen, he was well equipped to edit an important review dealing with a variety of subjects, some of them very ticklish. Although he had many enemies in his work who kept meticulous watch over every word he wrote or said, his orthodoxy was never once called into question or even suspected. This shows M. Portal to have been a theologian, though without advertising the fact. Rather like Pascal's honest man whose 'philosophy was to laugh at philosophy'.

The purpose to which he had dedicated his life and the important problems to which it gave rise, necessitated M. Portal in a close study of certain questions, and firstly that of ordination. The problem was what authority has the Church to modify, not indeed the sacrament itself, but its accompanying rites, even fundamental ones? He would recall that the theory of matter and form was only an application of the ontological hypothesis of the middle ages. He would cite the case of Durandus, Bishop of Mende, who introduced the tradition of the instruments, as an instance which showed how wide a Bishop's powers then were. From the sacrament of orders he would advance to confirmation, a sacrament which has undergone great changes as to its matter. As regards the eucharist he was much interested in the question of the epiclesis or invocation of the Holy Ghost at the time of the consecration. As is well known this question gave rise to serious controversy between the Greeks and the Latins. Anyhow, as M. Portal with his usual common-sense would say, it is neither arguable nor has it ever been seriously argued that the Greek mass is not just as valid as the Latin one. He liked taking a broad view of things rather than subjecting them to the subtle analysis characteristic of so much Western scholasticism. He attached great importance to the 'intention of the church', a subject which he thought merited the most careful examination of both the historical and the theological problems it raised. The defenders of the validity of Anglican Orders based themselves on this doctrine of the intention of the Church. M. Portal's personal opinion was that their validity was doubtful.

Apart from the sacraments, the problem of the Church was one which first arose when the Anglo-Roman movement started. What is the Church's authority, and in whom by divine law is it vested? This naturally brought M. Portal to the study of the position of bishops, who are the true successors of the Apostles, consecrated by the Holy Ghost, by no means merely papal *aides-de-camp* or apostolic executive officers. Historical study showed him not only examples of a great degree of autonomy in the episcopate but even among simple diocesans; the view that they represented and were responsible for not only their own diocese but the whole episcopate and indeed the whole Church. Closer historical study would show, he thought, that schism and even excommunication did not wholly destroy the feeling that all belonged to the one Church.

In addition to the question of episcopal authority, many questions arose on that of the Pope. M. Portal's faith in the dogmatic definitions of the Church were firm and without reservation, but he did not, like Ward, hope 'to find the announcement of a new dogma every day on his breakfast plate', nor did he favour a purely dialectic and syllogistic argument for the great privileges which have been granted to the Supreme Pontiff. He was opposed to any separation of the head from the body, the Pope from the Church. It was this which, from the first, he sought to make clear to his Anglican friends: that the papal prerogatives exist for the Church, are a function of the Church. The infallibility of the Pope is nothing other than the infallibility of the Church. It was by concentrating on this line of approach that he got learned and loyal Anglicans to say that on this there might be after all some agreement.

As in the case of the episcopate so in that of the Papacy, one must distinguish between the underlying God-given principle and the various historical developments. In the history of the Church there developed metropolitical and patriarchal Churches and so the Pope, Bishop of Rome and Supreme Head of the Church, had become also the patriarch of the West. His rights as such must be carefully distinguished from the privileges derived from his primacy. Also the political and social developments of the middle ages had given political powers to the Pope, both as sovereign of the Papal states and supreme arbiter between Christian monarchs. This too needed to be studied independently of the Pope's spiritual authority. This temporal power, resulting from historical circumstances, had undoubtedly had many bene-

ficial results, but it had also, owing to the many scandals
and abuses which had occurred, opened the Church to
serious criticism. This was readily admitted by M. Portal
as indeed by all competent historians. The continued life
and development of an organism such as the Church needs
a certain evolution. M. Portal did not disagree with this
opinion, at that time in great vogue, but he added the following interesting proviso : the classical analogy of the seed
which, without changing, grows into the tree quite different
in appearance, seemed, if not inexact, at least incomplete.
He would point out that in life, especially the life of ideas,
there can be both progress and regress, so might not a dogma,
having once developed, so to speak hibernate and be less
clearly appreciated than formerly ? So he thought that the
papal primacy had been more clearly perceived by the Church
in the first centuries than at the end of the middle ages at the
time of the famous councils of Basle and Constance. One of
his most fervent wishes was for a sound theological doctrine
of the Church : this he mentioned frequently. 'What we
need', he would say, 'is a really good treatise on the Church.'
An interesting attempt at this which gave M. Portal much
pleasure and greatly struck him, was a paper read to the
first congress of Velerhad in Moravia in 1907, by the Rev.
Father John Urban, S.J., entitled 'De eis quae theologi
catholici praestare possunt ac debent erga ecclesiam russi-
cam'.

This paper, which was extremely well received, was
highly critical of the opinion 'that no schismatics, any more
than heretics, belong to the body of the true Church of
Christ'. Such a theory would put an end to any question
of reconciliation of the Churches. Individual conversions
would be the only thing and 'we can imagine the effect of
such language on the Orientals by imagining it applied to
us if the Heterodox treated us as outside the Church of
Christ'. While retaining the idea of Christ's mystical body,
theologians had since the sixteenth century insisted on the
purely 'hierarchical' tie as the necessary basis of the Church's

unity, hence 'they regarded as outside the Church not only heretics but schismatics and any excommunicated person'. But Cardinal Franzelin—basing himself on the views of an old school of theologians, such as Cano and Juan de Torquemada, that what unifies the Church is baptism—regarded all baptized persons though outside the Roman communion, as members of our Holy Mother the Church, not indeed in the external forum but in the internal forum, and in God's sight, so long as they were in good faith. In Father Urban's view, however, this was not going far enough; he thought that 'the true function of the sacraments was to bring those already marked with the invisible chain which bound them, to the organic unity of Christ's mystical body. The character given by baptism is the primary and fundamental means by which the body of the Church is established and continues. It follows that no validly baptized person can in this life be completely cut off. Good deeds and habits, including even faith, are not so much part of the structure of the mystical body as results flowing therefrom. They are referable to its life and functions : contrariwise their absence does not necessarily involve that the member is wholly cut off; it is more productive of a fatal illness, a kind of paralysis.'

So we can regard even Protestants as members of Christ's mystical body. As to members of the orthodox church 'by virtue of the episcopate and priesthood which exist in their communion, they are in the body of Christ. Not as independent bodies but as already organized members, although not fully connected with the centre of the organism.' Father Urban concludes that this line of approach involves certain modifications of the current teaching on the 'notes' of the true Church, especially as regards Eastern Churches. It would be impossible to maintain that they were wholly lacking in apostolicity, holiness, and unity. Rather than denying to them any of the elements of the true Church, a more profitable argument is that as now situated, they lack those which can only be and ought to be supplied by union with the Roman Pontiff. The theory of the four 'notes' as an argument to be used with genuine seekers, is rather out of date : there are other more direct ones. However, even these are by no means compelling. 'Those Christian bodies which are separated from Rome and especially the Eastern are sufficiently part of the Church to secure salvation. Anyhow, there are many, both the simple and the learned, including theologians, who remain devoted and convinced members of their Church. Those whom God wills to bring to recognize the Roman primacy, He leads by different ways, varying according to the person's character, education, etc., which cannot be fitted into tidy compartments.' What are the objective tests for deciding whether a particular religious body is fully part of the Church demands a careful historical study of the constitution of the Church.

This paper of Father Urban's greatly interested M. Portal, who saw in it an outline of the treatise on the Church of which he dreamt. He published a résumé of it in one of the last numbers of *Revue Catholique des Églises*.

M. Portal's whole life's work was centred in the Church. It was at the centre both of his spiritual life and of his instructions. Nor is it possible to think of the union of the Churches or of any attempts thereto, separately from M. Portal. He has left no text-book, but he did better than write, he lived the theology of which he dreamed. Himself inspired by faith and charity, he believed that the Church's finest task was to win the world in the spirit of love and unity. All her organizations, however necessary to her earthly existence, lacked meaning and usefulness apart from this supreme ideal. To him, union and reform were equivalent : not only must any spiritual growth encourage a burning desire to heal the rents in Christ's mystical body, but no true union can come without such inner growth, a 'revival' as the English call it. Christians must get nearer to Christ before they can hope to get nearer to each other. What power, too, would flow to the Church from such unity ! M. Portal's method was very different from the usual : he always began by seeking points of agreement rather than points of disagreement. It is easy to write books to prove one's opponents wrong, but that kind of controversy has always dug more ditches than it has crossed. The better way towards union is surely to approach others, not as opponents but as separated brethren, recognizing and acknowledging such spiritual graces as they possess, which may indeed often enrich our own. Not all difficulties are thereby solved, and many questions remain to be answered, but a foundation has been laid, a foundation on which much may be built because it is based not on abstract ideas but on life — that is to say, on love, a love which will surely end in union. It is good to seek to convert individuals, but to unite whole families of mankind in faith and in love is an even nobler task. It is a task to which Cardinal Mercier unhesitatingly gave his warm approval. Few men can have brought about as much understanding and appreciation of Catholicism as did M. Portal. All who came into contact with him, whether non-Roman Christians or persons with little or no religion felt a personal attraction which benefited the Church to which he belonged. He was fully aware of this, and it was a source of great joy to him in the midst of the many disappointments he suffered. Nicolas Nicolaiovitch Nepluyef had said, when on his deathbed, that he was more fortunate than Moses, who had not entered the promised land: he had lived in the community. At the end of his life, M. Portal could well have said the same. Although he never saw complete unity achieved, he had tasted its first fruits and experienced the joy of a friendship devoted to serve this cause.

CHAPTER 8

M. Portal and Russia

M. PORTAL's attention had early been drawn to Russia by both his French and English friends. Foremost among the latter was Mr. W. J. Birkbeck, a great friend of Lord Halifax and like him a keen worker in the cause of Christian union. Mr. Birkbeck probably knew Russia better than anyone else; he spoke the language, travelled extensively in Russia, and had a large circle of Russian friends. He was on terms of friendship with the Imperial family, and had been given a special seat in the Cathedral on the occasion of the Tzar's coronation in 1896. He was interested in all Eastern Church matters, especially literature, and had translated into English the Russian Contakion for the departed which was performed in St. George's Chapel, Windsor, at the memorial service for Alexander III, a gesture greatly appreciated in Russia.

While M. Portal's friends Eugène Tavernier and Henri Lorin were introducing him to the writings of Soloviev, Birkbeck drew his attention to another great Russian thinker of fifty years earlier, Khomiakoff, one of the founders of the Slavophil movement. He had published his correspondence with a Deacon of the English Church, William Palmer, who had at one time thought of joining the Orthodox Church but eventually became a Roman Catholic. Birkbeck had probably influenced the Abbé Morel in his choice of Khomiakoff's writings for his introduction to Russian theology. He had also given Morel letters of introduction, which secured him meeting the most interesting of St. Petersburg's society, while Henri Lorin had commended him to some big noise in the police through whom he was received by Sabler, the procurator of the Holy Synod. As a result of Birkbeck's introduction, Morel had become on intimate terms with Khomiakoff's family, and it was while visiting his son Dmitri at his home at Bogoutcharovo near Toula, that Morel was drowned bathing in a lake. Apart from some entries in his diary referring to his journey he left behind a few theological essays, and, in addition, a very interesting letter addressed to General Kireiev which defines admirably the position of the Eastern and Western Churches, as well as suggesting positive means for their reconciliation. What were Abbé Morel's last thoughts on this ? A few days before his death he had written, 'My stay in St. Petersburg has not produced the results of which we dreamed. I have not found the man of requisite calibre and I wonder whether anywhere in Russia we can find the necessary outlook.' His Moscow friends had noticed that he appeared depressed, disposed to abandon his work in Russia, which they attributed, in part anyhow, to his great physical fatigue. Morel's death was a blow. A year later M. Portal sent to Russia a layman who was connected with the country through his mother's family, with a view to his becoming acquainted with the position and re-establishing the contacts which Morel had made. The next winter this layman contributed a number of striking articles on the soul of Russia.

During the summer of 1906 I decided to try to learn Russian ; [1] at the time I was not very keen on it, but the memory of Abbé Morel urged me at least to try to continue the work which he began. In the result I was pleasantly surprised, as the language proved not nearly as difficult as I had anticipated. Also it seemed to me that the Russian mind revealed a conception of life of great importance to the study of the Church and to the possibility of reconciliation. Shortly before the start of the holidays of 1907 M. Portal sounded me as to whether I would agree to spend them in Russia. On my answering that I would, he introduced me to Mr. Nicolas

---

[1] At this point in the original the author, the Abbé Gratieux, starts to write in the first person, and I have kept to this.—A. T. M.

Nicolaiovitch Nepluyef. This was a most remarkable man, a wealthy aristocrat who would have been completely at ease in any court or embassy, but who had devoted his considerable wealth and his estates in Tchernigov to founding a community or confraternity for Christian education and betterment of the people. One felt that here was a prophet speaking, when he told of how mysterious inner voices had revealed and called him to his vocation, which had led him some twenty years earlier to create the organization which he named 'The Workers' Confraternity for the Exaltation of the Holy Cross' and in which he had been joined by his mother and two sisters. He dreamed of extending the confraternity to include all Russians and even to countries abroad. Perhaps not wholly daydreams, as the big community at Vozdvijensk, which had been fully established, was in the framework and control of the Orthodox Church. At the outbreak of World War I it comprised some 1200 persons of all ages, which shows the responsiveness of Russians.

We were all enormously impressed by the accounts of the confraternity. He, on his side, was delighted at the welcome he received from M. Portal and his friends whose name and efforts towards reunion came to be highly prized at Vozdvijensk. Although the Workers' Confraternity was far from representing all Russia, it offered a congenial centre from which to try to get to know both the people and their ideas on reunion. No theological approach was possible as the confraternity looked upon the question in a way theologically unacceptable to both Catholics and Orthodox. They would willingly have agreed to a form of intercommunion incompatible with any doctrine of the Church. One day, without any thought of becoming controversial, I tried to raise with Mr. Nepluyef the question of the Church and asked him whether he did not think that the fruitful approach would be the study of the early centuries when the Church was still united. His reply was that he feared I was embarking on a false scent and would undo any good that I might do. 'History proves nothing,' he said, 'nothing matters but a living love.' I naturally said no more, but Mr. Nepluyef was more than his theology, and further, was a devoted son of the Church. He did over-emphasize the gifts of grace at the expense of the priesthood in a way which worried the authorities, especially Pobedonostser, the Procurator of the Holy Synod. This last had indeed thought out an ingenious way of regularizing the situation ; the appointment of Nepluyef as Bishop of Tchernigov, so making him the legitimate spiritual head of his own confraternity. But Nepluyef refused the position which, he said, would merely make him the tool of the Procurator. His vocation was to work as a layman and for that he had been blessed by a holy man renowned for his sanctity. The affection felt by the confraternity for M. Portal never cooled and his friends were always welcomed at Vozdvijensk.

It was Mr. Nepluyef who introduced me to Khomiakoff's son, Dmitri Alexievitch, with whom Morel was staying when he died. Mr. Nepluyef had also met in Paris a Russian scholar, the Abbé Oger, who was most enthusiastic over the work of the confraternity and expressed a wish to translate the complete works of Khomiakoff into French, giving the profits to further the work at Vozdvijensk. There was, however, some confusion because when Nepluyef met Khomiakoff in St. Petersburg he obtained his permission for me to translate his father's works, a thing which had never crossed my mind. This finally settled the direction of my work and introduced me into the small but very interesting circle of the adherents of the Slavophil movement in Moscow: Dmitri Khomiakoff and Theodore Samarine, the nephew of George Samarine, who was as proud of his uncle as Dmitri Khomiakoff was of his father. The Slavophil movement was nationalist but an idealist nationalism. They dreamed of the world-wide triumph of true Christianity, the establishment of which was, they said, Russia's vocation. 'My father', said Dmitri Khomiakoff, 'used to say that the division of the Churches was the greatest misfortune which had befallen mankind.'

However, in the full study of the Eastern and Western civilizations and of their differences, we came to appreciate what was the line of approach which the Easterns regarded as most likely to result in a lasting union. Men like Dmitri Khomiakoff and Theodore Samarine did not then realize as did Lord Halifax that Rome must be the centre and capital of a Christian world, but they were men with whom one could freely embark in the fullest and frankest discussions, hoping that one day a measure of agreement might be reached. One felt that in this direction as in the direction of England, something might be accomplished, and it gave M. Portal great joy to feel that at least contact had been established with Russia.

I kept in touch with Dmitri Khomiakoff and started studying the eight large volumes, both prose and verse, which contained the literary works of his father, Alexis Steponvitch Khomiakoff. This taught me much more of his thought than his French theological pamphlets. According to him the essential quality of the Church was a life of holiness expressing itself in brotherly love. Emphasis on the external organization leads to formalism and utilitarianism which, according to him, characterize the West. This theme is, of course, exaggerated and somewhat prejudiced. It is, however, a point of view which needs careful study, and I decided to write a thesis on this great Russian thinker. In the meantime I wrote some articles in the *Revue Catholique des Églises* on this and on Nepluyef's social work in his confraternity. The *Revue* was devoting more and more space to Eastern questions. Towards the end of the year there were published some excellent articles by Father Palmieri, one of the most knowledgeable of Catholic priests in Russia. A Polish priest wrote an answer to Father Palmieri which delighted M. Portal, who thought that a good controversy would be an excellent stimulant. About the same time he was following with interest the views being put forward at Congress of Velerhad in Moravia, formerly an archiepiscopal seat and the site of the tomb [not yet identified] of St. Methodius, the brother of St. Cyril and with him the apostle of the Slavs. Regular meetings of those learned in matters of the Church, of Slavism, and of the East had been arranged. In the early years there were many distinguished orthodox theologians mixing with the Catholics and many interesting and learned papers were read, including one on the Epiclesis by Father Maltsev, priest of the Russian Church in Berlin. These did not escape M. Portal's notice, and an interesting article on the first Congress of Velerhad appeared in the *Revue des Églises*.

M. Portal did not disguise from himself the difficulties surrounding the attempt to get nearer together, not least of which is the mixing of politics and religion. It is easy enough to stir up old prejudices, rivalries, ambitions among Russians, Poles, and Ukranians. Anyhow, Russians find it hard to believe that any meetings are for other than political purposes. One of them writes :

It is naturally always a good thing for people to get to know each other better, but I think that no practical result is possible unless based on complete mutual love, in the setting of the faith. I do not at all mean that those about to meet at Velerhad are not actuated by the feeling of mutual benevolence, which is a prelude to charity, but one gets the feeling that what is chiefly being sought is a sort of accommodation, of compromise rather than a spontaneous effort after unity, which alone can be effective. Russians remain highly suspicious of the word 'Union'. If the only discussion has been on how to unite separated bodies I doubt whether any solution is possible ; the only result might be to provide some more effective propaganda. But will any propaganda lead to real union or merely to one party scoring over the other ? In the religious and political sphere the West, up till now, has always regarded the East as a proper subject for conquest : had the view changed, the West's method of approach to us would have been quite different.

The author of these passages, Mr. Dmitri Khomiakoff, did not include M. Portal among the suspected Westerners. Following a visit from Mr. Birkbeck he wrote : 'Birkbeck

has somewhat opened my eyes to what kind of man is the
Abbé Portal. I should much like to meet him, could he not
some day come out as far, say, as Scythia.' A little later
Lord Halifax's book on Anglican Orders gave him a further
insight into M. Portal. 'From what you told me I formed
a very favourable impression of M. Portal, but thanks to
Halifax's book I feel an almost personal acquaintance with
the worthy man.' Khomiakoff's ideal was 'to obtain a
comprehensiveness which would include East and West,
while each should keep its peculiar characteristics'.

The growing attempts at a deeper understanding of Russian
life and thought could have been described and discussed
most usefully in the *Revue Catholique des Églises*, but, alas, the
time had come when it had to cease publication! Far from
being discouraged, M. Portal strove even harder to foster
vocations to Russia. His hospitality was offered to any young
men who were not afraid of the difficulty of learning Russian.
He would arrange their stay in Paris, their journey and even
their stay abroad. In this he got help from the new contacts
he was always making, among others from the Assumptionists
who were then, as now, doing fine work in Russia — in Kief,
Odessa, Vilma in the Donetz basin and now in Moscow. A
young Serbian monk who later became a bishop was studying
in Paris. He used to visit M. Portal and was captivated by
him. Long after leaving Paris he kept up correspondence
with 'his kind friends in Paris'. As he wrote from Geneva,
'I don't want my leaving France to end our friendship'. He
made known to his friends abroad both our work and the
occasional pamphlets describing it. On one occasion he
wrote, 'At the moment our common task for the union of all
who believe in our Saviour's redemptive work, which our
Lord commissioned us to do, seems to have been stopped,
but we can continue to prepare for a more favourable occasion. The Lord will not desert us.' The criticisms and re-
proaches of carefully planned propaganda in Russia, which
were then being made by the Orthodox, were a great grief to
our Serbian friend. In connection with the Congresses of

Velerhad, which the Archpriest Maltsev had attended against much friendly advice, he wrote :

What finally convinced Maltsev that he should suspect these brotherly neighbours was the Jesuits' propaganda in Moscow : Vertsinski's part in this and his German propaganda, also the Catholics' own private quarrels and their own admissions of a host of absurdities, and the malicious attitude towards the Orthodox. Those who are against the meetings at Velerhad had a further triumph when it was proved conclusively that the Metropolitan of Lwow had several times come secretly to Moscow to encourage the illegalities of the propagandists. Naturally Maltsev cannot defend Cheptitski, but can only regret ever trusting him.

The above shows what a delicate task is the attempt at union and how amply justified was M. Portal's approach, all to be done in perfect love and trust. Everyone trusted and confided in him : the same friend writes again, 'I have the happiest memories of M. Portal. I wrote two articles on his work for our paper, also one on the Abbé Morel. Both produced a very good impression.' On another occasion we came near to sending someone to Bulgaria, but Paris was the real centre of the work and of M. Portal's influence. It was there that he sent his young friends to M. Boyer's lectures and tried hard to get the Catholic Institute to start Russian classes. I think it true to say that without at all ignoring the Western philosophy which he recommended students to study, he had a leaning towards that of the Slavophil movement. He was very pleased that one of his young friends began studying the works of Tchaadaiev who, in one of his well-known articles, written in what the Russians called the thirties, taught the need to get to know Catholic Europe and to unite in a world-wide civilization. This thought of Tchaadaiev had been partly taken up by Vladimir Soloviev in his book *Russia and the Church Universal*. M. Portal in the lecture he gave at Louvain, in 1925, said of his work :

The love of Russia, of Holy Russia, stands out a mile, but the Papal rights are examined with a marvellous insight into the

constitution of the Church, [and again] the union of the Churches
was uppermost in Soloviev's mind, it was this which brought him
near to Stroosmayer, the great Bishop of Diakorov and apostle
of Slavonic unity.

M. Portal would have liked to find some writer to answer
Soloviev. He was not at all satisfied with the work of Father
d'Herbigny, especially its subtitle, 'A Russian Newman',
which he thought entirely inappropriate. According to
Tavernier, Soloviev had never ceased to believe that the
Russian Church was a true branch of the Church universal,
although he had recognized a formal primacy of Rome.
This view agrees with the apocalyptic sense which ends
Soloviev's 'Three Interviews', and also explains how he
came to receive the sacraments at the hands of an Orthodox
priest from Ouskoe just outside Moscow.

M. Portal kept abreast of practically all modern literary
tendencies. For instance, Merijkovski had visited him in
Paris and sent him a presentation copy of the book, *The
Tzar and the Revolution*. But the teaching of Merijkovski,
Hippius, and Dmitri Philosophoff was no possible basis for
the union of the Churches, and was quietly put aside. Every
kind of Russian called on M. Portal, who, although ever
gracious and kind, was much too wise to be fooled. Some
even professed a wish to join the Church of Rome, and
although M. Portal as a conscientious Catholic priest would
never refuse help to any who came to him, he did not think
that individual proselytizing was part of his work. At the
beginning of the twentieth century, especially after the 1905
revolution, there was much talk of reforms being about to
take place in the Russian Church : reform of the hierarchical administration, of the clergy, convents and seminaries.
There was speculation as to whether a council of all the
Russias would be called and a Patriarch appointed. M.
Portal followed all this closely, but as he no longer had the
Revue des Églises he had to try other ways of keeping the
French informed, and it was through him and Mr. Tavernier's

help that the *Univers* published a series of articles I wrote on the present situation of the Russian Church. It would have pleased M. Portal to see the Catholic Church and especially the French Church, with the experience she had of her own reform, offer help and advice to the Russian Church. In this, one recognized the true son of St. Vincent of Paul and the apostle of unity waiting patiently for his dream to come true. Our best Russian friends thought the same. 'The nearer we are to Christ the nearer we will be to one another.'

PART THREE

THE MALINES CONVERSATIONS

CHAPTER 9

The Malines Conversations—Death
of Cardinal Mercier

PRELIMINARIES AND FIRST CONVERSATION

THE reunion of the Church of England with the Catholic
Church had never been absent from M. Portal's thoughts.
His correspondence with Lord Halifax would alone have
kept it before him, and he himself still regretted his failure
to bring together theologians truly representative of the two
Churches. In 1896 his chief aim had been to promote
friendly talks between them, without any idea of indulging
in controversy or trying to get quick results. He had chosen
the question of Anglican Orders solely with a view of
interesting Anglicans in the idea of reunion and the possible
means of realizing it. He had no idea that the Sovereign
Pontiff, who then seemed much attracted by the Eastern
Church, would show so much interest in and desire for the
conversion of individual Anglicans to the Catholic Church.
M. Portal had greatly regretted seeing the project which was
so dear to him being shelved, and all interest concentrated
on the question of Anglican Orders: a question which was
bound to give rise to very violent opposition among English Catholics as well as offending Anglican susceptibilities.
How then did it come about that, after twenty-five years,
M. Portal got the idea of approaching Cardinal Mercier to
try to get support for his favourite idea from so eminent a
quarter? He had probably told Lord Halifax, his lifelong
confidant, of his project, but in the timing of this new
attempt is seen M. Portal's genius. He also happened to
have been in correspondence with the Archbishop of Malines

over a pamphlet he had written about the Sisters of Charity.
The Cardinal had thanked M. Portal for the presentation
copy he had sent him, and wished success to the work.
Thus it was, as M. Portal writes, 'in some respects under the
auspices of St. Vincent' that he ventured to draw the
Cardinal's attention to the important Lambeth Appeal of
1920, which ran as follows :

> The times call us to a new outlook and new measures. The
> Faith cannot be adequately apprehended and the battle of the
> Kingdom cannot be worthily fought while the body is divided,
> and is thus unable to grow up into the fullness of the life of
> Christ. The time has come, we believe, for all the separated
> groups of Christians to agree in forgetting the things which are
> behind and reaching out towards the goal of a reunited Catholic
> Church. . . . It is through a rich diversity of life and devotion
> that the unity of the whole fellowship will be fulfilled.

M. Portal was grieved by the lack of interest which Catholics
seemed to take in what he regarded as a remarkable step by
the established Church, and it then occurred to him to write
to Cardinal Mercier drawing his attention to the Lambeth
'Appeal'. This seemed to him to open the way to preliminary conferences which might well result in 'reordination', and he suggested that the Catholics should take the
initiative in suggesting them, as it was Leo XIII who first
thought of it, and had himself suggested Brussels as a
possible venue.

M. Portal was delighted to learn, in a letter he received
from Malines dated 3 February 1921, that the Lambeth
Appeal had not escaped the notice of the Cardinal,[1] who
had the feeling that here was 'something to be accomplished,
very circumspectly but in the spirit of Christian charity'.
He did not relish the idea of a conference, probably doubting
whether it could be arranged, but he promised to pray and
to seize any opportunity which might occur. There the
matter would probably have rested, had not M. Portal and

[1] It had, in fact, been sent to him by the Archbishop of Canterbury.—
A. T. M.

Lord Halifax visited the Cardinal at Malines, which they did after making a tour of the battlefields. At first he expressed some surprise, and asked Lord Halifax, not unnaturally, why he did not address himself to the English Catholic authorities. When Lord Halifax explained that there was a lack of sympathy in that quarter, supporting this from his personal experience, the Cardinal agreed to conversations taking place in his palace with a few representatives of the English Church. He regarded these as purely fact finding, in which the parties should try to discover upon how much they were agreed : the question of what publicity should be given to the meetings was not discussed.

A date was made for the first meetings at which the Cardinal had with him Mgr. Van Roey his Vicar-General, and M. Portal, while with Lord Halifax were his two friends, Dr. Armitage Robinson, Dean of Wells, and Dr. Frere, Superior of the Community of the Resurrection, Mirfield, afterwards Bishop of Truro. Before leaving London the three Anglicans met at Lord Halifax's house in London to agree on the basic points on which they must stand.[1] They did not regard Anglicanism as a mere federation, nor did they come to make a simple submission to the Church of Rome, but looked for a reincorporation of parts into a friendly body, larger and richer than any of the existing parts : in other words, a policy of mutual enrichment, and it was in this spirit they sought to examine old controversies. They regarded as essential all doctrines contained in (i) the Creeds (Apostles and Nicene), (ii) the catechism preparatory to Confirmation and first Communion, (iii) the Holy Scriptures as interpreted by the Church, (iv) the Prayer Book, and (v) the dogmatic decisions of the first six General Councils.[2] It was also mentioned that Catholics tended to

[1] This 'Outline of Points' is printed in Frere, *Recollections of Malines*, 1935, pp. 63-67.
[2] The 'Outline of Points' stated that Nos. (iii), (iv), and (v) were 'less explicit' than Nos. (i) and (ii). Also No. (iii) runs 'as interpreted by the Church *and the Catholic doctors*'. Frere, *op. cit.* p. 65. (Translator's italics.)— A. T. M.

multiply doctrines which they regarded as 'fundamental', whereas Anglicans tended to aim at a minimum.

The first meetings were held on 6, 7, and 8 December 1921. They were quite informal, there being no agenda, but many subjects were touched upon. Lord Halifax had prepared a Memorandum[1] to serve as a basis for discussions. It covered a large number of subjects; the nature of the Church, and an enumeration of the sacraments, Baptism, Confirmation, Eucharist, and Penance. But none of these were fully discussed as they would have been in any detailed comparison between the statements of Anglican teaching and the decrees and canons of the Council of Trent. The reading[2] of the Memorandum formed the basis of much discussion on points of detail. The Dean of Wells (Dr. Robinson) said he could not reconcile the Thirty-nine Articles with the Council of Trent, although Dr. Pusey and Bishop Forbes[3] of Brechin had not regarded them as insuperable obstacles to the reconciliation of the two Churches. The Anglicans were very anxious to know in what way a truth could become an 'article of faith' in the view of the Catholics. They (the Anglicans) did not recognize as ecumenical either the Council of Trent or the Vatican Council — at neither of which they were present.

The Catholics explained that the infallibility does not separate the Pope from the Church, and that he is the organ of the Church who can act for it without necessarily consulting its members. He does not put forward a new dogma, but merely declares explicitly and authoritatively what is already implicit in the Christian revelation.

As regards the Eucharist, the Anglicans relied on the official teaching, that in the Sacrament of the Lord's Supper

[1] Copies were circulated beforehand to those taking part in the meeting. Halifax, *The Conversations at Malines: Original Documents*, 1930, p. 10. The text of the Memo. is printed at pp. 71 *et seq.*—A. T. M.

[2] It was read by Cardinal Mercier: see Halifax, *op. cit.* p. 10 : Frere, *op. cit.* p. 22.—A. T. M.

[3] Alexander Penrose Forbes (1817–1875), Bishop of Brechin. Author of, *inter alia*, *An Explanation of the Thirty-Nine Articles*, 2 vols., 1867–1868, which was written at Pusey's suggestion.—A. T. M.

the body and blood of Christ are, through the consecration, verily and indeed taken and received by the faithful. The Catholics did not think it opportune at this stage to discuss at all fully the doctrine of transubstantiation.

The day of 7 December was given up to the Lambeth Appeal, which was read aloud. The Catholics refrained from commenting on many statements it contained, but when it came to Chapter VI Cardinal Mercier remarked that the Scriptures could not be regarded as the 'ultimate standard of faith', since these had to be interpreted by a living Church. Chapter VIII, which was of especial interest to Catholics, was then read. We give it *in extenso* :

We believe that for all the truly equitable approach to union is by the way of mutual deference to one another's consciences. To this end, we who send forth this appeal would say that if the authorities of other Communions should so desire, we are persuaded that, terms of union having been otherwise satisfactorily adjusted, Bishops and clergy of our Communion would willingly accept from these authorities a form of commission or recognition which would commend our ministry to their congregations, as having its place in the one family life. It is not in our power to know how far this suggestion may be acceptable to those to whom we offer it. We can only say that we offer it in all sincerity as a token of our longing that all ministries of grace, theirs and ours, shall be available for the service of our Lord in a united Church.

It is our hope that the same motive would lead ministers who have not received it to accept a commission through episcopal ordination, as obtaining for them a ministry throughout the whole fellowship.

In so acting no one of us could possibly be taken to repudiate his past ministry. God forbid that any man should repudiate a past experience rich in spiritual blessings for himself and others. Nor would any of us be dishonouring the Holy Spirit of God, Whose call led us all to our several ministries, and Whose power enabled us to perform them. We shall be publicly and formally seeking additional recognition of a new call to wider service in a reunited Church, and imploring for ourselves God's grace and strength to fulfil the same.

This constituted — for no other interpretation seemed possible — a definite offer by the Anglicans to accept (assuming the doctrinal difficulties overcome) reordination in the interests of peace and unity. It is true that the last part of the chapter, which appealed to the non-episcopal bodies to receive episcopal ordination, seemed to contain an expression of faith in the validity of their actual ministry : none the less it was true, as one of the Catholic members [1] of the conference said, that, 'considering the feelings at the time of the controversy about Anglican Orders, no one would have thought that such an offer would be made so soon after their condemnation. The action of the Anglican Bishops was a remarkable example of Christian humility and a real sacrifice in the cause of unity.'

At the first meeting there were discussed (in addition to the Lambeth Appeal) the Anglican conception of the Church, the Prayer Book doctrine of the sacraments, the place of Holy Scripture in relation to the Church's faith, and of the episcopate and the Papacy in the life of the Church, as well as the suggested reordination. The meeting was purely exploratory : its net result was to confirm the Cardinal in his belief that such private conversations were useful, both for making clear to each side the views of the other and for strengthening the desire of both for reunion. He thus recorded his impression of the meeting.

The first conference, which was quite informal, filled us all with a deep feeling of mutual esteem, of confidence in one another, and of brotherly cordiality, and it quickened our common desire to help forward, if possible, such a *rapprochement* as was desired by the Lambeth Conference, and as is desired now, perhaps more than ever before, by all those who have to look on, pained and often powerless, at the demoralization and even dechristianization of society.

More than a year was to elapse before this small group again found themselves at Malines. It is true that, in January 1922, Cardinal Mercier, in a letter to M. Portal, referred to

[1] It was M. Portal : see Halifax, *op. cit.* p. 24.—A. T. M.

'this first meeting which was a prelude to the further ones for which we hope'. However, that year was a busy one for the Cardinal, one of the most important events being the conclave which elected Pius XI in succession to Benedict XV.

In March 1922 the Cardinal addressed a Pastoral Letter to his flock, containing a long explanation and commentary on the significance of the conclave. Very soon after Lord Halifax published a pamphlet, 'A Call to Reunion', which contained a complete translation of the Letter, and was prefaced by an extensive Introduction, which ended with a new appeal for reunion:

The Cardinal, in the eloquent passage with which he concludes his Pastoral Letter, reminds us that the union of Christ with us, and of us with Him, which our Lord likens to the union which makes Him one with the Father, is the ultimate source and expression of Christian life and unity. May the Great Head of the Church so inspire Pius XI, that under the guidance of the Holy Spirit, Who alone can make men be of one mind in an house, he shall so work and pray that there may again be one fold and one Shepherd.

And shall we not also work and pray that we and our separated brethren may be once more knit together in one Communion and fellowship in the mystical Body of Christ our Lord? Imagine what it would be if in our day we might see its accomplishment. The vision of such a reunion is so transporting that all else fades into insignificance in comparison. What would its realization and the knowledge that it was no longer a distant prospect but an accomplished fact, be for us? Let us, then, pray to God with an earnestness which will take no denial, and with an absolute determination that our prayer shall be granted, that, with our own eyes, we may be allowed to see the representatives of a reunited Christendom, from East and West, from North and South, gathered in S. Peter's to offer, with one heart and soul, the holy, immortal, and all-prevailing Sacrifice by the hands of Pius XI, in thanksgiving to the Father of all for having, in response to their prayers, given again to His children the blessing of peace.

This pamphlet contained the first public disclosure that

such meetings had taken place and the hopes to which they gave rise. Cardinal Mercier took no further step until he had informed the Vatican, from whom he received, from the start, both encouragement and a blessing for the future. Equally Cardinal Bourne was kept informed: also the Archbishops of Canterbury and York evinced great interest and approached Cardinal Mercier with a view to increasing the number of Anglican representatives. Again in the same year the new Pope, Pius XI, published an Encyclical, 'Arcano Dei', which contained a definite appeal for reunion, and was a great encouragement to those who had been working for it. The Holy Father wrote:

From this Apostolic centre of the fold of Christ Our look turns next to the many who, either not knowing Christ or not fully holding His teaching or the unity established by Him, are still outside the fold, though destined for it by Divine Providence. The Vicar of the Divine Shepherd cannot but repeat and make his own the words which, with their simple brevity, are redolent of love and tender pity: 'Them also (the other sheep) must I bring', and must rejoice, too, in the happy prophecy of Christ Himself 'And they shall hear my voice, and there shall be one fold and one shepherd'.

SECOND MALINES CONVERSATION

The second conversation, with the same participants as the first, was held on 14 and 15 March 1923. Although they remained private, the authorities on both sides knew and formally approved of them.

At the request of the Anglicans discussion of doctrinal differences was postponed, and consideration given to the practical question of methods by which, assuming agreement on doctrinal points to be reached, the Anglican Communion might be brought into communion with the Roman Church. Anglicans naturally attached great importance to this matter in view of their devotion to their Church and to all for which it had stood for three centuries. They drew attention to the fact that there are now 368 dioceses in the Anglican Communion, as against 21, all in England, at the beginning of the sixteenth century. The Memorandum, which had been prepared by the Anglicans and a copy sent in advance to the Cardinal,[1] was taken paragraph by paragraph, so that its claims should be clearly understood. It is true that 368 dioceses acknowledge Canterbury as the centre of the Anglican Communion, but those dioceses outside England have considerable freedom in choosing their bishops, whereas English diocesan bishops are appointed by the Crown, which in practice means by the Prime Minister. Neither the Cathedral Chapters nor the Archbishop of Canterbury have any legal rights in the appointment of bishops : the Chapters receive a '*congé d'élire*' the person named, which they invariably do. To the Cardinal's question as to the exact position held by the Archbishop of Canterbury in the Church of England, the Anglicans answer that he is the Metropolitan and, as such, has effective canonical jurisdiction in his Province of Canterbury. He is the nominal head, or centre of dioceses outside England : he invites their bishops to meetings, *e.g.* the Lambeth Conference, at which he presides. He can also advise them, but has no power to give orders. In the view of the Dean of Wells reunion should be of the whole Anglican Communion with the Church of Rome.

How to reconcile the Pope's jurisdiction with the English principle that no foreign authority has jurisdiction within the realm proved a difficult question. In particular, even if other difficulties to reunion were overcome, how could the Pope have a voice in the appointment of Anglican bishops ? Neither the Cardinal nor M. Portal would admit the possibility of excluding all papal right of intervention, but the Dean of Wells thought that this might be done if the Archbishop of Canterbury were treated as a Patriarch, a position which could be recognized by a General Council.

[1] For full text of Memorandum, see Halifax, *op. cit.* p. 79 ; also Frere, *op. cit.* p. 31.—A. T. M.

The Catholics were very reticent on all questions put by the Anglicans. Even where they were inclined to agree, they did not feel at all authorized to make concessions. It was clear, however, that agreement could probably be reached on the two questions of the use of English in public worship and communion in both kinds. But they thought that Rome would probably be less accommodating on the question of clerical celibacy. The Anglicans recognized the theoretical advantages of celibacy, but opposed it being made obligatory.

INTERVAL BETWEEN SECOND AND THIRD CONVERSATIONS

There was a fairly long interval between the second and third conversations,[1] due primarily to certain misgivings among the Anglicans, not least the Archbishop of Canterbury, as to the results of the second conversation. The word 'pallium' was misunderstood at Lambeth, and the references to it were looked upon as a serious concession to the Catholics. Nor was uneasiness lessened by the action of the second Anglo-Catholic Congress, held in July 1923, in sending telegrams to the Pope and to the Orthodox Patriarch of Constantinople. Dr. Gore,[2] who had, in Advent 1922, preached three sermons criticizing the Roman claims from the Anglican point of view, wrote to the Archbishop, 'the concessiveness of our delegation to Malines, apparently at the first conference and certainly at the second, seems to be more disastrous and perilous the more I think of it'.[3]

Also the choice of additional delegates to the Anglican group was not an easy one. Whereas in 1895 Dr. Benson, then Archbishop of Canterbury, had seemed quite uninterested in the discussions in Rome on the validity of Anglican Orders, the present Archbishop (Dr. Randall Davidson) took

---

[1] It was eight months.—A. T. M.

[2] Charles Gore (1853–1932), Founder of the Community of the Resurrection, Mirfield; Canon of Westminster; Bishop, successively, of Worcester, Birmingham, and Oxford, which last he resigned in 1919.—A. T. M.

[3] G. L. Prestige, *Life of Charles Gore*, p. 480.

a keen interest in the Malines talks — though he remained very much in the background, and at first had refused to be involved officially. He was a personal friend of both the Dean of Wells (Dr. Armitage Robinson) and Father Frere, C.R. (Superior of the Community of the Resurrection, later Bishop of Truro), and it had been at his request that they accepted Lord Halifax's invitation to take part in the conversations. But after the incidents created in England by the second conversation, the Archbishop became very anxious as to what might be the outcome of future understandings between Anglicans and Catholics. Further delicate questions were being posed, and the Archbishop would probably have preferred that the next conversation be restricted to generalities, leaving, for the moment, discussion of the really vital questions. But Frere was very anxious that the question, really crucial for the Anglicans, of the position of the Pope in the Church should be discussed. The Catholics regarded Frere as almost one of themselves, so great was his subtlety of argument and good-will towards them, but Frere himself realized how necessary it was, in loyalty to the Anglican faith, to repudiate any claim that the Pope's authority over the Church existed *jure divino*, justifying every papal intervention in the life of the Church. This is clearly brought out in a letter he wrote to Lord Halifax on 12 December 1922.[1]

The Archbishop seemed rather to favour the restriction of discussion at the approaching meeting to general questions, leaving the other matters for later consideration. On this I disagreed with him. It seemed to me that we had finished with general ideas, and that we must now have a more specific agenda.

I did not persist further on this : as personally I am clear that in our next programme we should accept the challenge of the Cardinal's pastoral letter, and come to the question of the Papacy. We must put all our cards on the table, and set out all our objections. I see these as following naturally on what the

[1] The original of this letter having been impossible to trace, I have retranslated it from the French translation in Hemmer's *M. Portal*.—A. T. M.

Cardinal has said; and it seems to me that having at the earlier meeting shewn a certain degree of friendship, goodwill and moderation (I hope so at least) the time has come for us to shew a little of our obstinacy, and to make them understand (what they don't seem to have appreciated) the strength of our position as against that which they regard as secured, especially by the 1870 Council.

I think we were well advised not to touch on this subject the first time, but I cannot but think that it is necessary to come to it now. In fact, after what the Cardinal has said in his pastoral letter, and what you have written, I think we must come to grips with the essential problem, although I do not see any way in which we can solve it satisfactorily one way or the other.

Dr. Armitage Robinson, the Dean of Wells, was a great scholar and a loyal Anglican. He was highly regarded by the Archbishop, who had wanted him as one of Lord Halifax's colleagues, and had no intention of dropping him from the subsequent meetings. Frere was possibly more sympathetic towards Rome and more inclined to recognize that she had acquired, largely through force of circumstances, rights under ecclesiastical law. But neither would admit that such existed by divine law. Dr. Robinson's position is shown clearly in the letter he wrote to Frere on 12 February 1923.

I think that the 21st is the day to begin our preliminary meeting, and I will come to London then, if that is agreed between you and Lord Halifax.

It would be of great advantage if you could outline beforehand the lines you think we might adopt. What is the leading Principle? How many Bishops had we when the breach with Rome took place? How many are there in Communion with Canterbury today? Must not Canterbury be regarded now as a quasi-Patriarchate, with a fuller measure of independence than France or Spain could reasonably ask?

We cannot be controlled by a set of Italian Commissions prompting the orders of a Pope. Our first question then must be, Will such a position as I have indicated be for a moment considered by Rome? If not — if Cardinal Mercier thinks it could not — I do not think I could go to Malines.

If you think well, will you send this on to Lord Halifax with your own view on the point which I have raised. Also let me hear from you.

Lord Halifax, the third of the original Anglican representatives, was also a friend of the Archbishop, who although he might not himself have selected him as representative of the Church of England in discussions like those at Malines, had complete confidence in his loyalty and did not hesitate to confide in him his fears concerning the future of Anglicanism, as appears from his letter dated 20 March 1923.

I realise the immense care and anxiety which you with the Dean and Frere took to reach some position which might give a standpoint for further progress in the direction of the solution which you have so eagerly desired. My own desire for it is as keen as your own, though I think the difficulties loom larger to me than they do to you. Perhaps it would be more true to say that you have faith which removes mountains. I have felt it to be right to address a letter to the Dean of Wells, a copy of which I enclose to you. It was written after full discussion with him and with Frere, and both of them desired that such a letter should be written. Robinson has not yet seen it, but Frere has, and approves of it as laying emphasis on the need of caution in the future and the danger of misunderstandings arising. I fear I must hardly anticipate that you will regard it as quite in accordance with what you would have wished, but you have throughout shown so friendly and helpful a spirit towards myself that I am hopeful you may not object to it even if you wish that it had been worded a little differently. I have tried to word it in such form as not to give legitimate pain to our Roman Catholic friends, while at the same time I have felt bound to say honestly what I do feel (and what I am certain the majority of our people in Church and State feel even more strongly) about the danger of our seeming to acquiesce in a recognition of what I regard as the untrue Papal claim.

That Lord Halifax was entirely worthy of such confidences is also clear from the following two letters written to him by Dr. Gore, who was not only the Archbishop's right-hand man, but also the farthest from Lord Halifax in his views and hopes. They are dated the 24 January 1923 and the 1 April 1924 respectively.

You are an old and great friend and I love and honour your character. But you know there have been always between us great differences by reason of temperament — such as may well subsist between people who are at one in catholic faith and practice — such as make argument as futile as it is distasteful. My desire is to work for union among Christians wherever it seems possible. I see many possibilities of union among Protestants as in Scotland. For us I see great possibilities of union with the suffering Orthodox. I do my very best to promote it. Towards Rome I can conceive a small section of Anglicans being reconciled. But those whose principles (as it seems to me) should admit of it, do not appear to me to desire it. Even if they believe Roman doctrine, they dislike or fear Roman authority. As for the mass of the Anglican Church, it seems to me that it is mere wilful blindness to think of reunion as possible within the present horizon. As for the proposed conference, I can conceive nothing more healthy in its effects than a plain statement such as Figgis would have made, and such as my little book will contain, of how we regard Rome — viz. as a very onesided development of Christianity into intellectual and moral despotism. It is only to say how profound must be the reformation of Rome before union would be possible. I imagine that my little book is just out. Certainly I have no intention of withdrawing it. Let us be friends in spite of differences. But I want you to recognize the differences.

P.S.—I gather you mean me to keep the Pope's Encyclical. But a p.c. shall fetch it back if you want it. I will read it — in fact I have read it almost all.

To me the failure of the Papacy to bear its witness first against Germany at the outbreak of the War — then against the spirit of the Treaty of Versailles or the spirit of France — and more than anything else its attitude towards the Orthodox Christians and the way it has lent itself to facilitate the weakening of the Orthodox Church and the extirpation of the orthodox in

Russia and the Near East constitute one of the most lamentable instances of failure on the part of the most powerful Church in Christendom that the world has ever seen.

My dear, very dear, Halifax,

It is good of you to have taken such pains, with so courageous a hopefulness, to get me into the right way. But I fear it is quite out of my power to go the way you point. I have for 45 years or more realized my differences — different differences — as from Liddon, so from you. We must be content to be thankful for our large measure of agreement. I do not think anything would be gained by arguing. I can only assure you I have written with as much desire to know the truth and further the purpose of Christ as possible. It is not your way to be interested in a great deal that to me is very important.

You know that I am not at all disposed to ignore or minimize Anglican deficiencies. But that is no reason for voluntarily taking upon ourselves the defects we have not got.

You speak of my being an obstacle to a 'reunion of the Episcopate', i.e. the Anglican with the Roman. Do you know a single English Bishop who would by any persuasions of mine be led in that direction except after a profound change in Roman dogma? Surely the most you could, with the utmost sanguineness, hope for, on your terms would be the formation of a Uniat English Church consisting of at most a few hundred priests and a few thousand people; and what would that do for the cause of Reunion? To my mind I fear that nothing presents itself as so great a hindrance to the Catholic movement in the C. of E. as a whole as the utterances of those who have been speaking in your sense.

There is no use in our quarrelling or arguing. It is only your indomitable and youthful hopefulness carried to excess which explains your letter.

Once the Catholics and Anglicans had decided to increase the number of their respective representatives, the choice of the Anglicans proved a difficult matter for the Archbishop of Canterbury. Two names suggested themselves: Dr. Gore and Dr. Kidd, Warden of Keble College, Oxford. The latter was an authority on ecclesiastical history and the author of a three-volume history of the early Church, down to the Council of Chalcedon, and he had also made a special study of the Reformation period. His choice was welcomed by Anglicans. The majority also welcomed the choice of Dr. Gore, whose reputation as a scholar was second to none. He was well known for the part he played in the publication of *Lux Mundi*, as well as being the author of many theological and historical essays. His views were not wholly agreeable to the more extreme High Churchmen (of whom Halifax was one), especially in view of his outspoken criticism of the Roman claims (see *supra*, p. 132).

Meanwhile the Archbishop had, on his own account, recorded his views in a Memorandum, the essential part of which reads as follows :

It ought to be made clear on the Anglican side, beyond possibility of doubt, that the great principles upon which the Reformation turned are our principles still, whatever faults or failures there may have been on either side in the controversies of the sixteenth century. It would be unfair to our Roman Catholic friends to leave them in any doubt as to our adherence, on large questions of controversy, to the main principles for which men like Hooker or Andrewes or Cosin contended, though the actual wording would, no doubt, be somewhat different today. What those men stood for we stand for still ; and I think that in some form or other that ought to be made immediately clear.[1]

Some of the High Churchmen disliked Dr. Gore's apparent agreement with the Archbishop. For instance, Dr. Frere, in a letter to Lord Halifax of 28 January 1923, following on some outburst of Dr. Gore's, wrote :

It is sad to have this sort of division at home ; but I think inevitable and it may in some way under God's hand help on the cause. Rome has two things at least to learn (a) the strength of our Anglican case which it does not realize or even suspect as yet and (b) the enormous difficulties that our well-founded prejudices make in all sections of English Churchmanship.

[1] Frere, *op. cit.* p. 77. This was read to a group of Anglican divines by the Archbishop at Lambeth on 2 October 1923. Frere, *op. cit.* p. 40.—A. T. M.

They must come to see that the inheritance of hatred and suspicion affects many of our best English Catholics as well as the Evangelicals and the man in the street : and Gore's outburst will be a eye-opener to many. I do not say that this justifies it. We need the spirit which recognizes in Rome, even regarded as the enemy, a growing willingness now to amend its ways as well as much done in that direction these 300 years. We ask them to see how we have changed and are changing : and we must get our people to see the same in them : and it is sad that Gore should not lead in that direction but in the opposite.

But I believe that it and much more will be overruled for good if we go on quietly and faithfully.

Gradually, however, Lord Halifax came to realize the advantage which Gore's massive learning would bring to the meeting at Malines.

The Archbishop was sufficiently anxious about the matter to write to the Cardinal explaining that certain interpretations of Papal Supremacy would be unacceptable to the Church of England and inviting the Cardinal's comments and explanations. The Cardinal answered by a letter[1] dated 11 April, the following extracts from which almost constitute a statement of the doctrine of the Papacy.

The logical train of our Conferences, as well as the mutual duties of loyalty on the part of the members who meet there, oblige us to take up again this examination of the primacy of the Bishop of Rome, successor of Peter, defined as a dogma of the catholic faith by the Vatican Council.

Our third conference, which like you I hope may be soon and, to a certain extent enlarged, will assume then the task of studying this doctrine more thoroughly, and will apply itself, in accordance with your desire, to making more precise its significance.

Meanwhile, I make it my personal duty to tell you what I believe to be the Roman Catholic doctrine on the special point about which you wish to question me.

You ask me if the Primacy accorded to the Sovereign Pontiff signifies or entails this consequence, that alone, by divine right, the Pope is the Vicar of Christ on earth, in this sense that from

[1] For full texts of letters, see Bell, *Randall Davidson*, pp. 1267 *et seq.*—A. T. M.

him alone derives, directly or indirectly, all legitimate power to exercise, validly, a ministry in the Church; 'If the term "primacy" is understood as implying that the Pope holds *jure divino* the unique and solemn position of sole Vicar of Christ on earth, from whom as Vicar of Christ must come directly or indirectly the right to minister validly within the Church'.

Certainly the Pontiff of Rome is, in a special sense, the Vicar of Christ on earth, and the piety of the faithful is accustomed to bestow on him this title by choice. But St. Paul states that all the apostles are the ministers of Christ; '*Sic nos existimet homo ut ministros Christi*'. The Roman Liturgy, in the Preface to the Mass for Apostles, calls all the apostles the 'Vicars' put in charge, by the Eternal Shepherd, of the pastoral direction of his work: '*Gregem tuum, pastor aeterne, non deseras, sed per beatos apostolos tuos continua protectione custodias: ut iisdem rectoribus gubernetur, quos operis tui Vicarios eidem contulisti praeesse pastores*'. Still more, of the simple priest in the exercise of his ministry, we say readily that he is the representative of Christ, 'another Christ', '*sacerdos, alter Christus*'. If he did not occupy the place of Christ, '*vices gerens Christi*', '*Vicarius Christi*', how could he truthfully say of the Body and of the Blood of our Saviour; '*Hoc est Corpus meum; hic est calix Sanguinis mei*'; how could he, in remitting sins, which God alone can absolve, say '*Ego te absolvo*', 'I absolve thee'?

The ordinary application of the title 'Vicar of Christ' to the Sovereign Pontiff does not involve therefore as a consequence, that *alone* the Bishop of Rome possesses powers coming direct from Christ.

The powers of the Bishop refer for one part to the Body, real, historical, of our Lord Jesus Christ — 'Power of Order' — for the other part, to his mystical Body — 'Power of Jurisdiction'.

The power of 'Order', power of consecrating the Body and Blood of our Saviour in the Holy Eucharist, power of conferring on someone else the fullness of the priesthood, including in that the ability to transmit it with a view to perpetuating the Christian life in the Church, was given by Christ to all his apostles. It belongs fully to the bishops, their successors, inalienably; no human authority whatever could break its validity. Is it not well known, for example, that the Church of Rome recognizes the persisting validity of the Orders and Sacraments in the

Eastern Orthodox Church, which, nevertheless, has been separated for a thousand years from the Roman Primacy?

The power of 'jurisdiction' power of ruling the Church, the mystical body of Christ, belongs by divine right to the episcopate, that is to say to the bishops, successors of the apostles, in union with the Sovereign Pontiff. The episcopate, regarded as the whole institution of government, is of divine right and it would not be in the power of the Bishop of Rome to abolish it.

The power of 'jurisdiction' devolved upon each bishop is also of divine right; it is ordinary and immediate within the limits of the diocese assigned to the bishop by the Sovereign Pontiff.

The peace and unity of the Christian Society demand, in fact, that at the head of the government of the Church there should be a supreme authority, itself ordinary and immediate, over the whole Church, over the faithful and their pastors; to this supreme authority belongs the prerogative of assigning to each bishop the portion of the Christian flock which he is called to rule in union with the Pontiff of Rome and under his authority.

The bishop's power of jurisdiction over his flock is of divine right, but when the theologians ask how this divine origin ought to be interpreted, their counsels are divided.

One party holds that this power of jurisdiction comes immediately from God, like the power of 'Order'. According to this conception, the Pope nominates the bishop, assigns to him his subjects, but the jurisdiction over these subjects comes from God, without human intermediary. This opinion, in the words of Benedict XIV, has on its side solid arguments, '*validis fulcitur argumentis*'. But, he adds, to this opinion is opposed another, according to which the jurisdiction comes from Christ, as principal source, but is granted to the bishop through the intermediary of the Roman Pontiff. According to this conception, episcopal consecration gives to the bishop the qualification for jurisdiction, but the actual complete jurisdiction is dependent on the mandate of the Sovereign Pontiff.

This opinion, says Benedict XIV, seems to have on its side better arguments of reason and authority: '*rationi et auctoritati conformior videtur sententia*'.

No further decision, which commands universal assent, has

settled the controversy. Neither does the *Codex juris canonici* edited by Pope Benedict XV, the word of which is law in the Catholic Church, settle it.

It sums up in these words the general doctrine of the Roman Church concerning the episcopate : '*Episcopi sunt apostolorum successores atque ex divina institutione peculiaribus ecclesiis praeficiuntur quas cum potestate ordinaria regunt sub auctoritate Romani Pontificis*'.

This universal authority of the Sovereign Pontiff, say the Fathers of the Vatican Council, ought not to be considered by the bishops as a menace or a danger. It is, on the contrary, for the authority of the bishop over against his flock, a support, a strength, a protection.[1] More than once, in the course of my episcopal career, my experience has confirmed the truth of this conciliar declaration.

But this is not the time for me to enlarge on this subject. I must confine myself to replying briefly to the question about which your valued letter has engaged for a moment my attention. The conference, which we shall, shortly, please God, have occasion to resume, will have to examine more closely the question, which surpasses all the others in importance both christian and social, of the Primacy of the Pope.

This answer somewhat reassured the Archbishop, who finally chose Dr. Gore as a representative, which provoked the following, 'He [Davidson] endeavoured to prevent anything like dramatic agreement by the selection of Dr. Gore, who of all Anglo-Catholics is perhaps the most definitely anti-Roman'.[2] In accepting the invitation, Gore wrote to the Archbishop on 31 July 1923 :

I think it is of such immense importance — with a view to your retaining your present position in real mental vigour as

[1] In the Cardinal's letter there follows a quotation from chapter 3 of the Constitution 'Pastor Aeternus', of which the following is the English translation :
'But so far is the power of the Supreme Pontiff from being opposed to the ordinary and immediate power of episcopal jurisdiction, by which bishops, who have been set by the Holy Ghost to succeed and hold the place of the Apostles, feed and govern, each his own flock, as true pastors, that their episcopal authority is really asserted, strengthened, and protected by the supreme and universal pastor.'—A. T. M.

[2] Sidney Dark, *Archbishop Davidson and the English Church*, 1929, p. 201.

long as possible — that you should be relieved of any anxiety in whole or in part, that if you seriously believe my joining the party for Malines would relieve you, I cannot doubt that I ought to agree to go.[1]

The Catholics had also to choose two representatives, so as to keep the numbers even. M. Portal, in one letter, shows a preference for Father MacNabb, a Dominican of Downside, who favoured corporate conversion, adding, 'I wish the Dominicans would take some interest in the matter'. When, however, Father MacNabb was forbidden by his superiors to take part, M. Portal suggested the Abbé Hemmer, a learned French patristic scholar and Church historian : Cardinal Mercier at once agreed. The Cardinal also invited Mgr. Batiffol, another learned French scholar, who had been warden of the Catholic Institute for Girls at Toulouse, and was the author of a number of works on Church history, as well as on dogmatic theology. He had also recently been engaged in a sharp little controversy with Dr. Gore. He was a first-class scholar and a worthy opponent of Dr. Armitage Robinson and of Dr. Gore.

The correspondence between Lord Halifax and M. Portal during the interval between the second and third conversations, throws light on the motives animating the Archbishop of Malines. According to M. Portal he is sceptical of the reported change of attitude of Cardinals Billot and Merry del Val towards the Malines Conversations. If they are now favourably inclined to corporate conversion, why don't they write to the English papers to explain to the Catholics there their sudden change? Lord Halifax writes to M. Portal that Father Walker and a few others should be pressed to state their views in the Catholic Press, but that, as regards themselves, they must stick closely to Cardinal Mercier, whose integrity, under every trial, boundless charity, and ardent wish for their success, should be an inestimable help.

[1] Bell, *op. cit.* p. 1277.

The third conversation was held at Malines on 7 and 8 November 1923. The number of those taking part had been increased. In addition to the original participants there were, on the Catholic side, Mgr. Batiffol, a Canon of the Cathedral of Notre-Dame, Paris, and the Abbé Hemmer, then Vicar of Saint-Mandé, later Vicar of the Church of the Holy Trinity, Paris; and on the Anglican side, Dr. Gore and Dr. Kidd, Warden of Keble College, Oxford.

The high-light of this meeting was the Memorandum [1] written by the Dean of Wells, entitled 'The Position of St. Peter in the Primitive Church. A summary of the New Testament Evidence.' It can thus be summarized. St. Paul, in his letter to the Ephesians, enumerates the members and functions of the Church : its foundation is the Apostles and Prophets, Christ himself being the cornerstone. He does not mention St. Peter, on whom should rest the unity of the Church on earth. In the same way in the Epistle to the Galatians, St. Peter and St. Paul are on equal terms, the one the Apostle to the Circumcision, the other the Apostle to the Gentiles. The Acts of the Apostles also show St. Peter and St. Paul as equally prominent in the Apostolic band, though St. Peter sometimes carried out particular actions, but not on any recognized general authority to guide the Church's action. St. Peter is often named together with St. James and St. John, but without any special pre-eminence. The thrice-repeated question 'lovest thou Me?' (in St. John's Gospel) can be seen as a special charge to care for Christ's sheep, a duty imposed on him on the ground of his restoration from a specially grievous fall (the three-fold denial). Finally it is true that, in St. Matthew's Gospel, St. Peter has a special place in the functions of the Church; but the text 'Thou art Peter, and upon this rock I will build my Church' occurs only in this Gospel, and if St. Paul knew of it, he must have interpreted it in a sense which was not

[1] Printed in full in Halifax, *op. cit.* pp. 89 *et seq.*—A. T. M.

exclusive, but representative. The Dean admitted, however, that St. Peter often acted as spokesman or leader of the Apostles, though not their ruler.

In the afternoon Mgr. Batiffol read his reply.[1] He said that in his Epistle to the Ephesians St. Paul was describing the essential unity in Christ of all Christians, whether converted from Judaism or Gentility : he was not dealing with the unity of the Church in its concrete reality — its functioning. In the Epistle to the Galatians St. Paul does not mention James and John in reference to the Gentiles, to whom he has been appointed apostle. He says that the Dean ignores the rôle given to St. Peter in the First Epistle to the Corinthians. Nor is he right in his treatment of the Acts of the Apostles, where, although the technical words denoting supreme authority are not used, St. Peter acts as a real head of the Church, and is referred to as a person holding first rank, both in the New Testament and in the later tradition. On this question M. Loisy takes a more liberal view than the Dean : 'The basic authority of the apostles is not incompatible with St. Peter's particular authority, any more than that of St. Peter is incompatible with the authority of the apostles'.

In the summary [2] of the New Testament evidence as to the position of St. Peter, read by Dr. Frere at the morning session on 8 November, it was recognized that St. Peter was the accepted chief or leader of the Apostles, and was so accepted because he was treated so by our Lord, but that did not imply any jurisdiction held by him alone.

The Catholics maintained, on the contrary, that both the Acts of the Apostles and the Gospels show clearly Jesus's will to confer a special position on Peter, who is treated as the 'foundation and principle of unity of the Church'. The Vatican Council, when it defined the primacy and universal jurisdiction of the Pope, merely confirmed the historical facts as recorded in Scripture.

[1] Printed in full in Halifax, *op. cit.* p. 103.—A. T. M.
[2] Printed in full in Halifax, *op. cit.* p. 44.—A. T. M.

On 8 November Dr. Kidd read his Memorandum [1] on the position of St. Peter in the tradition of the Church. He dealt first with the tradition as revealed in the *Decretum Gelasianum*. According to St. Irenaeus the Roman Church was founded by St. Peter and St. Paul, and its bishop occupies the only known Apostolic See in the West. He has a primacy among all bishops of Christendom, so that, without communion with him, there is in fact no prospect of a reunited Christendom.

Mgr. Batiffol showed that, from the second century, the Roman Church is regarded as the foundation of the whole Church. Tertullian regards the Roman See as being that of St. Peter only, and from then all true Catholicism depends on the primacy of the Bishop of Rome.

In the afternoon Dr. Kidd read his second Memorandum. [2] It dealt with the repudiation, at the time of the Reformation, of the temporal and spiritual primacy of the Pope in the government of the Church of England. Such spiritual headship as exists involves constitutional and not autocratic power.

As regards the more modern pronouncements, the Abbé Hemmer did not deal with them, pointing out that they did not deal with St. Peter's commission; but he said that he proposed to treat of the relationship of the Popes with Bishops in a separate paper which he would prepare for the fourth conversation.

The Dean of Wells denied completely any universal jurisdiction, though he agreed that the Pope had a general superintendence, a 'spiritual leadership'. Dr. Gore preferred the expression 'spiritual responsibility'.

The importance attached to this third meeting is seen from the fact that the Archbishop of Canterbury, in a letter [3] dated Christmas 1923, addressed to the Archbishops and Metropolitans of the Anglican Communion, referred at

[1] Halifax, *op. cit.* p. 123; see also p. 47.
[2] Halifax, *op. cit.* p. 151.—A. T. M.
[3] For passages dealing with Malines, see Bell, *op. cit.* p. 1282: Frere, *op. cit.* p. 82.—A. T. M.

length to the Malines Conversations, which he said he had
followed with interest, without being himself responsible,
and from which he hoped for fruitful results. This carefully
worded statement caused a violent reaction in the religious
world, and provoked many comments, in differing senses, in
both Anglican and Roman Catholic papers.

The Times correspondent in Rome, in a dispatch dated
2 January 1924, stated that the Vatican neither knew of nor
had encouraged the Conversations, and that the Belgians
and French were not qualified for such an undertaking.[1]
It was probably this report which inspired the *Écho de Paris*
to publish an article expressing doubts about the usefulness
of the conversations, and the English Catholic papers, the
Universe and the *Tablet*, made the most of these pessimistic
rumours. Although Rome seemed unmoved by all this,
Cardinal Mercier thought it right to state publicly his responsibility in getting together, in his episcopal palace,
members of the Church of England and Catholic theologians.
This he did in a letter to his clergy, dated 18 January 1924.
He first stated how these meetings had come to be held, and
then their purpose.[2] It was clear, however, that the Cardinal was beginning to show signs of great fatigue.

However, M. Portal was able to pay him two visits
during that year (1924): the first on 19 June, the feast of
Corpus Christi; the second, in company with Lord Halifax,
at the end of November. The Cardinal had planned to stay
with his friend in Paris, at 14 rue de Grenelle, breaking his
journey to Rome in December, but an alteration in the
times of the trains prevented this visit taking place.

During this year between the third and fourth conversations, M. Portal not only kept up with his personal friends,
but was concerned to defend the principle involved in
Cardinal Mercier's words (from his letter to his clergy,
supra), 'I would not for the whole world tolerate that one of

---

[1] This correspondence was under the heading 'Christian Unity — Papal
views and the Primate's letter — Vatican and Malines Conference'.

[2] An English translation is printed in Frere, *op. cit.* p. 90.—A. T. M.

our severed brethren should have the right to say that he knocked trustfully at the door of a Roman Catholic bishop, and that this Roman Catholic bishop refused to open it to him'. It was on such lines that M. Portal answered the objections of those who criticized the policy of seeking corporate reunion.

The year 1924 saw the golden jubilee of Cardinal Mercier's priesthood, which caused great delight to his friends and disciples. On his return from the celebrations, M. Portal strove hard to encourage people to pray regularly for the success of their work. He well knew that it is God alone who brings any work to fruition, and throughout his life as apostle of union he tried to stir up regular prayer. It was through his efforts that the Whitsuntide novena (instituted by Leo XIII in his Encyclical *Divinum illud munus*) was always celebrated with great pomp in the Lazarist chapel, rue de Sèvres, near the remains of St. Vincent of Paul.

The year 1925 saw the publication of two Pastoral Letters on reunion, one by Mgr. Chollet, Archbishop of Cambrai, the other by Mgr. Ricard, auxiliary Bishop of Nice. Among the Non-Catholics was a Call to Prayer for reunion by Dr. Frere, Bishop of Truro, and a volume of meditations for the octave of Whitsunday, published by the 'Conference of Faith and Order'.[1] M. Portal published a charming article he wrote called 'Les Cloches de Soleure' in the *Revue des Jeunes*, expressing his great joy at this recrudescence of prayer.

THE FOURTH CONVERSATION

The fourth conversation was held at Malines on 19 and 20 May 1925.

Mgr. Van Roey read his paper on the 'Episcopate and the Pope viewed from the theological angle'.[2] In it he distinguished carefully between truths of the faith which

[1] The branch of the Oecumenical Movement which organised the Conferences at Lausanne in 1927 and Edinburgh in 1937. It is now absorbed in the World Council of Churches.—A. T. M.

[2] Printed in Halifax, *op. cit.* p. 159.—A. T. M.

have been defined, truths which are theologically sure, and matters which are open questions. It was an excellent statement of the Catholic teaching on the relationship between the episcopate and the Sovereign Pontiff, and on infallibility in the realm of doctrine. In the discussion which followed Dr. Gore remarked that while Mgr. Van Roey's paper stated clearly the theory of the episcopate, in practice the authority of bishops had been greatly diminished by that of the Pope. To this, Cardinal Mercier answered that never during the eighteen years he had been a bishop had he been thwarted by Papal intervention — not even during the war.

The Abbé Hemmer, replying to Dr. Gore and Mgr. Batiffol, who both raised the question of the canon law, said that as it was one of the Holy See's essential duties to provide against any unusual or unforeseeable eventuality, the Pope was not, in cases of necessity, strictly bound by the sacred canon law. The same consideration was the answer to Dr. Kidd's thesis (developed at the third conversation) that the Pope enjoyed a constitutional, not an autocratic headship. The Anglicans agreed that in the course of the Church's historical development the Roman See had acquired a certain 'primacy'; but they did not regard this as part of the divine constitution of the Church. In the course of history there had developed a body of ecclesiastical law which is contrary to divine law. The Roman Church has defined certain dogmas, *e.g.* the Immaculate Conception and Papal Infallibility, and cannot, therefore, admit that anyone can — *salvo jure communionis* — disagree with Rome.

In the afternoon the Abbé Hemmer read his paper on 'The Relation between the Pope and the Bishops considered Historically'.[1] In this summary he threw into high-light the occasions when the Bishop of Rome intervened in the affairs of the Church. One could not point to any particular moment in time when 'the Bishop of Rome was given a new authority, previously unknown, and the result either of the high-handedness of a usurper, or of the consent of some

[1] Halifax, *op. cit.* p. 187.—A. T. M.

assembly'. The needs of the times produced the changes in the Church's government, and any alteration in the relations between the Pope and the bishops was the result of God's guidance through the centuries.

Dr. Gore admitted that in many cases papal intervention had proved providential, but insisted that the Roman Church had lost many valuable critical and democratic elements which are retained in Anglicanism, Orthodoxy, and Protestantism.

On the following day, 20 May, much to the surprise of all present, Cardinal Mercier read a paper on the possibility of an Anglican Patriarchate, united to Rome, but autonomous.[1] The author was said to be a canonist, unnamed at the meeting, but later known to be Dom Lambert Beauduin, the Benedictine. According to him, by divine law all bishops, excepting the successor of Peter, Bishop of Rome, are equal, but by human or ecclesiastical law, either customary or positive, there exists a hierarchy — of patriarchs, primates, archbishops, metropolitans, etc. He thought that, before the Reformation, the Archbishop of Canterbury occupied a position very similar to that of a Patriarch, but so completely obedient to the Holy See that the Church of England became the most fundamentally Roman in all Christendom. Adopting the uniat principle of patriarchs, he put forward the idea of an association between the two Churches which could be regarded as union without absorption. The Archbishop of Canterbury would be re-established in his traditional position of Patriarch of the Anglican Church, whose organization would be remodelled on that of the Eastern Churches, and would have its own canon law and its own liturgy. The author went so far as to suggest that the Anglican Patriarch should take precedence over cardinals, except, perhaps, cardinal bishops.

The Anglicans regarded this Memorandum as too important to be discussed at once, and the Catholics were taken

[1] Halifax, *op. cit.* p. 241. The title is 'The Anglican Church united, not absorbed'.—A. T. M.

by surprise at the reading of what had not been previously circulated. "It was therefore agreed that the Memorandum should not be treated as one of the official documents of the 'Conversation'. When, later, Lord Halifax took it upon himself to publish it in his *Conversations at Malines: Original Documents*, not only did the Anglican members protest, but Mgr. Van Roey, then Cardinal Archbishop of Malines, wrote to the effect that the Catholics at the time expressed reservations and that the Memorandum was not to form part of the official documents.

Dr. Gore read a Memorandum on 'Unity with Diversity', which was first published in Dr. Frere's *Recollections of Malines*.[1] Basing himself on a sentence of St. Cyprian, he asks whether Anglicans and Catholics can differ on matters of doctrine without destroying unity between the Churches. He would like to limit doctrines necessary to be believed, to those which had, in substance, always been believed by the Church. He asked, 'Is the idea wholly impossible that, with a view to the corporate reconciliation of the Orthodox Communion and the Anglican Communion, the Roman Church could be content to require not more than the acceptance of those articles of faith which fall under the Vincentian Canon, which I am at present supposing to coincide with what Fr. Janssens recognizes as fundamental doctrines?'

At the next session's discussion Mgr Batiffol disagreed with the Protestant distinction between 'fundamental' and other doctrines. There was a long discussion on those truths which are fundamentally implicit, known more or less by process of inference. Those councils which are admittedly ecumenical have sometimes defined doctrines which clearly have been the subject of real development.

THE ALBERT HALL CONGRESS: THE WEEK FOR UNION

At the meeting of the Anglo-Catholic Congress held on 9 July 1925, at the Albert Hall, Lord Halifax made a speech

[1] Frere, *op. cit.* p. 110.

which, although expressing only his own views, was a striking declaration of his faith in the cause to which he had devoted his life. In it he recognized the primacy of the Pope to be 'divina providentia'.

In regard to our relations with Rome it is necessary for us to remember that the authority of the Pope (according to Roman teaching) is not an authority *separate* from that of the Episcopate, but when acting in full unison with the Episcopate, he is to be regarded as the centre and symbol of unity, invested, in virtue of his office, with Apostolic authority over, and solicitude for, the visible Church of Christ throughout the world.

It is well, therefore, to remind you that, although it may be difficult, if not impossible, to arrive at a rigorous delimitation of the respective rights *jure divino* of the Pope on one side and of the Episcopate on the other, reunion between ourselves and Rome is unattainable unless we are prepared to concede a primacy *divina providentia* as appurtaining to the Holy See, and to admit the claim of the Pope to occupy a position in relation to the whole Episcopate such as no other bishop can lay claim to. This is a matter which must be faced by us, with all its implications.

In his letter to M. Portal of 20 July 1925, Cardinal Mercier exclaimed, 'What a wonderful man is dear Halifax! At his age, to come forward as he did at the Albert Hall is really great! I cannot doubt that God will bless his great courage, which is inspired by his absolute faith.'

On the continent there was equal enthusiasm for the cause of reunion, and a 'Week for the Union of the Churches' was held in Brussels from 20 to 26 September 1925. This was a brilliant gathering, and speeches were made by Mgr. Izeptyesky, Fathers de la Taille, Tyzkiewez, S.J., Maniglier, O.A.A., and the Benedictine Dom Lambert Beauduin. Cardinal Mercier gave the final address, which he named 'Pour l'union des Églises', and in it he stressed the need for sympathy and prayer in the work of reconciliation of Christians.[1] M. Portal also spoke of the events of 1893 to 1896,

---

[1] The most important addresses were published in the *Revue Catholique des Idées et des Faits*, 23 October and 6 November 1925.

in which he played so important a part, and the results of which were so disappointing to him. He displayed no bitterness whatever, quoted Cardinal Wiseman at length, and ended with these words :

> We will fight and fall along with our brothers. We will fight and pray with God's Church in all confidence. Our path cannot be more difficult or discouraging than was that of the apostles, nor more thorny than that of our Saviour. 'The disciple is not above his Master.'

On 19 November M. Portal and Lord Halifax were together at Louvain, for the purpose of delivering an address on reunion to a Belgian Youth Conference. In it M. Portal defined, with outstanding clarity, the method of approach to his separated brethren which a Christian should adopt :

> The union of the Churches will be effected only through real apostles, men, that is, full of faith, making use of all supernatural means : prayer, from which all graces flow ; charity, by which we enter into communion with other souls, even when separated from us ; and humility, leading us to confess our sins and short-comings. We have all sinned against the Church : that is a fact which we must acknowledge.
> These, it seems to me, are the essentials of all work for reunion. Politics and politicians are outside these things : science is impotent, and a dilletante approach is sacrilege. Workers for union must be ready to toil, and to suffer.

He added a word, however, on the great help which friendship could be in so arduous a task.

> I would say to the young of today, and of tomorrow, that there exists a means of multiplying a hundredfold the strength of our efforts; a means essentially human, but ennobled, as all human nature is ennobled, by divine grace. I speak of friendship. A true friend is a gift from God, even where the sweets of affection are known in both joy and sorrow. But if we meet another soul at one with us in our noblest aspirations, whose ideal is to devote his life working for the good of the Church, that is of our Lord

and Master, Jesus Christ, to such a one we become bound in the very depths of our being. And if it should be that such Christians are separated by belonging to different Churches and to wholly different surroundings, but are determined to use all their energy to removing the barriers, and agree on a course of action towards this objective . . . think what power they can exert.

To illustrate the truth of this, M. Portal pointed to the friendship between Henri Lorin and Vladimir Soloviev, which was instrumental in producing Soloviev's *La Russie et l'Église universelle,* and to his own intimacy with Lord Halifax.

His speech at this meeting can truly be regarded as M. Portal's spiritual testament. In the evening of life, he casts a bird's-eye view on his apostolic ministry. From Madeira to Malines — with Rome taken on the way — he sees his life's work as a unity, ever inspired by his love for our Lord in His Church. Always and everywhere he has employed but this one weapon — an all-embracing sympathy and understanding, which were in great part revealed to him in the joys of a lifelong and enduring friendship. And this guiding principle, by which his life's work has for so long been guided, in spite of the many sorrows which it brings, he now seeks to pass on to the future apostles of union.

As an honest and conscientious labourer, M. Portal was satisfied with his work, as tending to hasten the coming of the Kingdom of God; and so it is with confidence that he now seeks to guide the young along the path he has trod. He ended his speech with these words :

Have faith, you young people. You are entering life at a time when great things are in store, especially in the religious world. In particular you will, maybe, witness the reunion of the Church of England with the Church of Rome. I ask you, when that day comes, to spare a thought for the two friends whose work and suffering had, in some measure, enabled you to gather the harvest.[1]

[1] See *Revue Catholique, etc.,* 11 December 1925, p. 5.

THE DEATH OF CARDINAL MERCIER

The last days of the year 1925 were saddened by the news of Cardinal Mercier's illness, which ended with his death on 23 January 1926. When it became clear that the end was near, both Lord Halifax and M. Portal travelled to Malines for their last visit to the great Cardinal. The following account of the last days is largely based on that written by M. Charles Mercier, the Cardinal's nephew.

Of all the visitors to the saintly Archbishop, Lord Halifax and his friend, M. Portal (those two great protagonists of the reunion of the Churches), were certainly the most welcome to his apostolic heart. Stirred by a feeling of saintly devotion, the Abbé Portal had hastened to the clinic, fully expecting to find his old friend there. In fact he got there one day before Lord Halifax, and saw the Cardinal alone on 19 January.

At this interview the future of the conversations was discussed; the Cardinal told M. Portal of the arrangements he had made for the eventuality of his death; gave certain instructions and much useful advice.

The next day his Eminence sent word that it would give him great pleasure if Lord Halifax and his friend would assist at the mass which would be celebrated in his room the next morning, Thursday 21 January, at seven o'clock. Lord Halifax, who was greatly moved, accepted the invitation with gratitude, and on the next morning, at the hour named, the noble old man and his faithful friend made their way to the clinic in the rue des Cendres. Lord Halifax went in first, crossed himself, and kissed the hand which the Cardinal extended to him. Canon Dessain then came in and began the mass.[1] It was St. Agnes' day. At the Agnus Dei, the saintly invalid put on his stole — symbol of the pastoral functions — to receive the Holy Communion, his last in this world. And while, in imitation of his divine

---

[1] There were present Brother Hubert, two sisters of the clinic, the Abbé Van den Houte, Lord Halifax, and M. Portal. See M. Portal's account in *La Croix*, 9 February 1926.

Master, the good shepherd offered his life for the sheep, a noble representative of the English Church, sunk in prayer, was uniting in spiritual communion with all Christ's followers.

After the mass and the recitation of the Litanies of Our Lady, the visitors made to leave the Cardinal alone for his thanksgiving, but seeing this, he sat up, opened his arms wide towards Lord Halifax, and in silence the two apostles of unity embraced.

The final Malines Conversations were held on 21 January. The doctors had been most insistent that the meetings be put off, as they feared the worst consequences from any prolonged effort. 'Never mind', said the Cardinal. 'We must meet.'

A first meeting was held at about ten o'clock in the morning, when the results of the previous meetings were gone through, and plans for their continuance discussed.[1] His Eminence spoke for about twenty minutes, in a firm and clear voice, evidently anxious that Lord Halifax should understand him clearly. He and M. Portal then retired to give the invalid some rest, during which time they agreed on certain proposals, on which unanimous agreement was reached at a second interview with the Cardinal. All present were astonished at the clarity of his mind, and his soul seemed endowed with a divine serenity.

When this talk was ended, the Cardinal expressed a wish to convey to the generous-hearted Anglican Archbishop of Canterbury his thanks for the messages of sympathy which had been brought to him by Lord Halifax. On that same day, after Lord Halifax and M. Portal had left him, he dictated the following letter[2] to his secretary:

Brussels, January 21
1926

MY LORD,

In the trial which it has pleased God to send me during these last weeks, I cannot express the pleasure and comfort it has given

[1] The next Conversation had been fixed for January 24.
[2] It is published in the original French, in Bell's *Randall Davidson*, p. 1299. —A. T. M.

me to receive a visit from our revered friend, Lord Halifax. He
has told me of the abiding desire for reunion by which you are
animated. I am made happy by that assurance, which fortifies
me at this present hour.

Ut unum sint, that is the supreme desire of Christ. It is the
desire of the Sovereign Pontiff; it is my desire; and it also yours.
May it be realized in all its fullness.

The proofs of sympathy that your Grace has been good enough
to have transmitted to me have touched me deeply. I thank you
for them with all my heart, and beg your Grace to accept the
assurances of my religious devotion.

When the time came to say farewell, the Cardinal asked
the saintly old nobleman to sit close beside his bed, when
he took both his hands in his own. He then took from his
finger his episcopal ring, and showing it to Lord Halifax,
said, 'You see this ring: it is engraved with the names of
St. Désiré and St. Joseph, my patron saints, also of St.
Rombaut, the patron of this metropolis. It was given to me
by my family when I was made a bishop, and I have always
worn it, although I have had others. Well, if I come to die,
I would like you to have it.' Lord Halifax, trembling with
emotion, made a gesture of protest: 'Yes, yes,' Portal inter-
jected, 'for you and for Edward'.

The Cardinal then gave a final blessing to Lord Halifax
and his family, and to M. Portal and his friends in Paris.
Then he suddenly remembered someone else — James, Lord
Halifax's faithful valet. 'Where is James?' he asked. James
was sent for, and the Cardinal blessed him too.

The final scene was thus described by M. Portal in *La
Croix*:

At 1.20 p.m. Lord Halifax, seemingly quite tireless, started
back for England, and I got to Paris later that day. Within
forty-eight hours, which was sooner than we had expected, the
Cardinal's great soul had returned to God. At the suggestion of
his confessor, Fr. Van den Steen, he offered his life for all those
objects which had been dear to him, especially the union of all
the Churches. On 27th January we were back in Brussels, Lord

Halifax being accompanied by Dr. Kidd, Warden of Keble College and one of the participants at the Conversations. These two represented the Archbishop of Canterbury at the Cardinal's funeral. The Abbé Hemmer and I represented the French side. Mgr. Batiffol was unable to be present.

It only remains to add that on the evening on which the Cardinal's obsequies were celebrated — 29 January, the feast of St. Francis of Sales — Madame Mercier, the sister-in-law of the deceased, with all her family, called on Canon Dessain to hand over to Lord Halifax the episcopal ring which the Cardinal had left him.

Lord Halifax kept this ring as a relic. He had an exact replica made, which he gave to Mgr. Van Roey, the Cardinal's successor in the see of Malines.[1]

Cardinal Mercier having died, the survivors thought that, though the conversations should continue, it would be well to draw up some statement of the results then reached, in view of the extent to which the Cardinal's personality had influenced them all. The need for some such had been foreseen by Cardinal Mercier himself, who refers to it in his long and beautiful letter to the Archbishop of Canterbury dated 25 October 1925.[2]

My dear Lord,

As soon as I received your letter of August 1st, I made a point of acknowledging it at once, but I found myself compelled to ask for some delay in order carefully to consider its contents. This delay has been prolonged far beyond my expectation. Being accustomed as you are to the difficulties of a great administration, I trust you will excuse me and forgive this apparent neglect.

When I first read Your Grace's letter it caused me some uneasiness. I was not sure that I had grasped its inner meaning. The document was inspired by an unaltered good-will, the esti-

---

[1] Until his death, Lord Halifax wore it on a chain round his neck. It was afterwards set above the base of a chalice and given by the first Earl of Halifax to York Minster, for use at Mass on the anniversaries of the deaths of Cardinal Mercier and Lord Halifax, and on St. Peter's day.—A. T. M.

[2] This is printed in both French and English, in the *Official Report of the Malines Conversations*, Oxford University Press, 1927, pp. 60 *et seq.* as Appendix III.—A. T. M.

mates of the past were encouraging, but the reflections on the present situation and on future developments seemed to betray some diminution of confidence. This was not surprising since, in so long and protracted an effort as ours, while the goal remains the same, the means to reach it will vary according to circumstances and raise new problems at every step.

In the course of our meetings, as the line of demarcation between the subjects on which agreement already exists or has been reached and the subjects in regard to which differences still exist becomes more distinct, the difficulties in the way of final success loom larger on the horizon, and the reasons for hoping seem less convincing.

On the other hand, when we listen to the voices on both sides of those outside our meetings, we notice a restlessness which it is not within our power to appease, and it may be that we, I mean your Grace and myself, feel some anxiety and weariness which it is not always easy to dispell.

Among our Roman Catholics, this restlessness assumes two aspects. Some of them, full of enthusiasm and sympathy for our cause, complain of our apparent dilatoriness and of a silence which seems to them unduly prolonged. They are inclined to imagine that the problem of reunion being stated, like a theorem of geometry, its affirmative or negative solution ought to be reached immediately. If the worst came to the worst, they say, a majority vote would put an end to all hesitations. They would like to see the Malines conversations proceed more rapidly and thus satisfy, without further delay, the curiosity of public opinion. The return of England to unity would be such a beautiful and edifying spectacle that the sooner it is effected the better for the sake of all the comfort that the religious minded would derive from it.

Others, on the contrary, influenced by the policy of 'all or nothing', consider only the final or total result, exaggerate arbitrarily the difficulties which must be overcome before that result is reached, and undervalue the supreme part played by grace in the evolution of spiritual life.

Relying only upon themselves and upon the knowledge of their own weakness, they would readily abandon at once an attempt in which, to tell the truth, they have never placed any confidence, and which perhaps, at the bottom of their hearts, they have never favoured, and for the success of which they have perhaps never prayed.

Your Grace must, no doubt, meet with the same restlessness on the part of inveterate optimists and obstinate pessimists among your own flock: they wish to obtain from us an immediate solution, and, if they could, they would urge us to end the matter promptly.

Does not Your Grace think that it would be weakness on our part if we gave way to these solicitations? We have responsibilities which our followers do not share and do not always understand. Our situation imposes upon us the duty to consider the general situation from a higher standpoint, according to standards more deeply supernatural. The direction of consciences entrusted to us allows us to act with authority.

Your Grace's letter mentions certain announcements which should be made, certain 'statements' in which the points agreed upon by the two sides should be definitely outlined and in which the points still under discussion should be recalled. I eagerly accept this proposal, and am ready to place it on the agenda of our next meeting, which might take place, as Lord Halifax desires, in the first fortnight of January 1926.

'Statements' might be prepared, the first on the conclusions already reached, the second on disputable points which have been partially considered, or on new subjects which, according to the wish of one or both sides, ought still to be placed on the agenda.

This comparative survey would show, I believe, that not only have our meetings brought hearts together, which is already a very appreciable result, but that they have also on important points harmonized our thoughts and achieved 'progress in agreement'.

The first 'statement' on common conclusions might either be developed in a more explicit form or be published in a concise form. It would be a happy means of maintaining the religious interest of our respective flocks.

In my humble opinion, however, it would be inopportune to publish any statement of disputable points. Negative conclusions, whatever they may be, would necessarily provoke polemics in the Press, reawaken ancient animosities and accentuate divisions, thus harming the cause to which we have resolved to devote ourselves.

In loyalty to our original purpose, we must bring to light progressively whatever favours reunion, and set aside or defer whatever stands in the way. Our original intention was not to examine, within a set time, a few questions of theology, exegesis, or history, with the hope of adding a chapter of apologetics or controversies to the scientific or religious works of our predecessors. On the contrary we met face to face, as men of good-will and sincere believers, alarmed by the confusion of opinions and the divisions of thought prevailing in modern society, and saddened by the progress of religious indifference and of the materialistic conception of life which follows it. We had in mind the supreme wish for reunion, for unity expressed by our Divine Saviour : '*Ut unum sint*'; 'That they may be one'. We set to work without knowing either when or how this union hoped for by Christ could be realized, but convinced that it could be realized since Christ desired it, and that we had, therefore, each one of us, to bring our contribution to its realization. Reunion is not our work and we may be unable to achieve it, but it is within our power, and consequently within our duty, to prepare it and *pave the way* for it.

Was it not for this high purpose that the Lambeth Conference was called together in a spirit of trust in the wisdom and goodness of Divine Providence? Is not this the unique object pursued for more than fifty years by our dear and revered colleague who devotes, with such admirable zeal, his time, his strength, and his heart to the cause of reunion?

I seem to hear the revered Dean of Wells addressing us in such moving words, at the close of our first meeting:

'For four centuries Anglicans and Roman Catholics were only aware of their antagonisms and divisions: they have met for the first time in order better to understand each other, to remove the misunderstandings which estrange them, to draw nearer to the goal so wished for by everyone — reunion.'

When the revered Dean uttered these moving words, he did not merely address our small and limited group but the mass of believers which we knew were behind us and whose perseverant faith in Christ and in the Church is the object of our constant care and anxiety.

As far as I am concerned, it is in this light of apostleship that I have looked upon my contribution to the conversations, from the first day when Lord Halifax and the Abbé Portal expressed the wish that I should join them. When, in January 1924, I explained to my clergy and to my diocese the part which I had taken in our conversations, I dwelt on the same point. I reminded them of the words of Leo XIII, 'The great events of history cannot be gauged by human calculations'. Foreseeing and fearing their impatience, I recalled to them the teaching of St. Paul on the unique source of the fruitfulness of apostleship : 'So then, neither is he that planteth any thing, neither he that watereth ; but God that giveth the increase' (1 Cor. iii, 7). And I added these words which I beg leave to repeat here : 'You are getting impatient, success is slow to come, your trouble appears wasted. Be on your guard ; nature and her eagerness mislead you ; an effort of charity is never lost.'

Reaper of souls, we must sow in the sweat of our brow, mostly in tears, before the hour of reaping strikes. When this blessed hour does strike, another very likely will have filled our place : 'Alius est qui seminat, alius est qui metit' (John iv, 38).

It is in this spirit of Christian patience and supernatural confidence that we shall meet again in January next, content to labour and to sow, leaving to the Holy Spirit and to the working of His grace the choice of the day and the hour for reaping the crop which our humble works and our prayers endeavour to prepare.

For this also and above all else we must declare : We associate ourselves as students, it is true, but our association is chiefly spiritual and joins in common prayer. The knowledge of our mere existence and of our periodical meeting is, for the general public, a constant exhortation to religious thought and collective prayer for reunion.

So M. Portal and his friends started arranging for a last meeting. It was fixed for August 1926, but was not in fact held until 11 and 12 October 1926, after M. Portal's death.

One of his last great joys was to follow the beginnings

of the building of the Benedictine monastery at Amy-sur-Meuse, in Belgium, which was especially dedicated to the work for reunion. But the greatest consolation of his last days lay in the memory of all the kindness shown to him by Cardinal Mercier. 'I have known sorrow,' he told a friend, 'but that is past. The Cardinal's friendship has amply repaid all my suffering.'

Nor did M. Portal regard the Cardinal's death as severing the ties which bound them, but believed that he was still praying for reunion. It was indeed some recompense to this faithful old servant of reunion, whose faith both in supernatural grace and in the power of personal friendship had never wavered, that, in the last years of his life, he was admitted to such intimate relationship with the saintly Cardinal. We cannot doubt that the two friends, now united in eternity, still help with their prayers those who humbly seek to continue their work.

FIFTH CONVERSATION : DRAFTING OF REPORT

When the conversation of May 1925 ended, the members had in mind to meet again fairly soon, in order to agree on a Report of the meetings up to date. As appears from his letter to the Archbishop of Canterbury of 25 October 1925 (*supra*, p. 158) Cardinal Mercier was anxious that any statement published should be restricted to emphasizing how the meetings had 'brought hearts together', and stating the points on which agreement had been reached; and so leave great hopes for the future. The death of the Cardinal, followed by that of M. Portal within five months, put an end to these projects.

It is probably true that, of the ten persons who met between 1923 and 1925, only Lord Halifax and M. Portal really believed in their heart of hearts that reunion, in the sense of the reconciliation of the English and Roman Churches, was possible. Possibly Dr. Kidd thought so, and the Cardinal certainly hoped for it. But throughout the conversations all tended to put forward their own theses, hoping that discussion would bring about mutual adjustments. So it was that between 1923 and 1925 much work was done of which it was difficult, at once, to assess the results, although the Catholic members acknowledged, to their own surprise that, in view of some of the Anglican statements, these were more definite than they had hoped.

On 11 October 1926 there met at Malines, Mgr. Van Roey, who had now become Archbishop, Mgr. Batiffol, the Abbé Hemmer, Lord Halifax, Dr. Frere, and Dr. Kidd. For two days they worked on the drafts of the Reports — one by the Anglicans, the other by the Catholics.

Dr. Armitage Robinson, Dean of Wells and formerly Dean of Westminster, was the principal author of the Anglican résumé. He was one of the most eminent scholars of the Church of England, and was respected and trusted by all its members. His Report, which had, of course, been criticized and modified by the other Anglicans, though it does not always do justice to the differing views of the Catholics, states the Anglican standpoint in authoritative and often remarkable terms. Especially in regard to the authority of the Holy See one detects a real effort so to state it that, without at all compromising the Anglican position, no sacrifice is made of essential Catholic doctrine. Dr. Robinson's Report on Malines takes us considerably further than the Oxford Movement.

The Abbé Hemmer was entrusted with the writing of the French Report, in which he set out the views expressed by the Catholics present at Malines, and emphasized especially the points on which the Anglicans were prepared to meet them. A comparison of the two Reports is instructive, and, especially in England, it acted as an opportune justification of the work undertaken by Cardinal Mercier, of blessed memory.

We print below that portion — section V — of the Catholic report[1] which deals with the Pope and his authority.

---

[1] *Malines Conversations, Official Report*, pp. 86 *et seq.*

With regard to the special position of the Pope in the Church, the divergences in belief and opinion are more serious and more difficult to reconcile. The Conversations at Malines, however, have given to the Roman Catholics an opportunity of explaining the precise meaning of their doctrinal statements in regard to the powers of the Papacy, and to the conditions under which these powers are exercised. The Anglicans, on their side, have expressed themselves in terms which, while not endorsing all that Roman Catholics believe and think, yet seem to us to justify a great deal of hope for the future.

His Eminence Cardinal Mercier himself introduced the subject in some degree, and he emphasised the impossibility that any society should exist without a head (*caput*). 'Even if we were to set on one side the proof which is drawn from Holy Scripture and tradition, in order to show that Christ definitely made the unity of His Church to rest upon the head of Peter and his successors, yet we could *a priori* maintain that Providence in its wisdom was bound to make apparent in one head the unity of authority in the Church. No doubt the episcopate might be a means of unification : but surely the bishops themselves, whose numbers in the course of several centuries must have risen to a thousand and more, are exposed to the danger of disagreement, just as priests are in a diocese, or parishioners in a parish. What then would be the factor of unity? Surely the one who in a family is called the father, and in a state the sovereign.'

In the course of an entirely frank conversation on this subject Anglicans and Roman Catholics expressed in common certain views, which we quote, either from propositions formulated by one or the other party, or else from explanations made by way of commentary. These, without in any way forcing their meaning, may be summarized as follows :

'St. Peter was accepted as chief or 'leader' because he was treated as such by our Lord.

The see of Rome is the only apostolic see known in the West. No Patriarchate has ever been established there side by side with Rome; and the Pope, according to St. Augustine's phrase in regard to Innocent I, 'presides over the Western Church'. The Church of England, in particular, owes its christianity to the Roman see, which, through the agency of St. Gregory, 'sent it baptism'.

Further, the Pope possesses a primacy among all the bishops of Christendom; so much so that, apart from communion with him, there is no hope or prospect of ever seeing a reunited Christendom. He occupies, in regard to all bishops, a position such as no other bishop can claim in regard to him.

From the first beginning of Church History there has been recognized to belong to the Bishop of Rome amongst all bishops a primacy and a power of general leadership.

Thus the primacy of the Pope is not merely a primacy of honour, but it implies a duty of solicitude and of activity within the universal Church for the general good, in such wise that the Pope should in fact be a centre of unity, and a Head which exercises an authority over the whole. It was, in fact, on many occasions due to the action of the papacy that the medieval bishops were able to defend themselves against the encroachments of the Civil Power. The papacy has been a guarantee of the spiritual independence of the Church.'

As to the manner in which the Pope has used his powers in the past, the Anglicans expressed various reservations. But they recognize that among their people there is needed much revision of opinion in regard to the Roman Church; in particular, as all agree, a recognition of the fact that the Roman Church reformed herself at the Council of Trent.

If an attempt is made to go further, as, for example, to sketch in definite outline the duties of the Pope in acting for the well-being of the Church Universal, and to undertake an enumeration of the corresponding rights, our Anglican friends show some unwillingness to go into detail.

It may, however, be useful to reproduce here some examples of the language they use. These are of great interest since they indicate an identical tendency of thought and a similar line of research, and thus they encourage the hope of a much greater measure of agreement in the future.

The exact phraseology is here of importance on account of the idea which underlies it. When they speak of 'spiritual responsibility', 'spiritual leadership', 'general superintendence', 'care for the well-being of the Church as a whole', their mind seems, throughout all such language, to fasten upon a very positive conception of a certain power, rich in its capacity but ill-defined in its extent. Memories of ancient times have left some bitterness of heart. It is better not to go back upon the past, but to try to forecast the forms which papal activity might take in the future. But what emerges from these expressions is the sense of a lofty mission attaching to the Pope, with the implication that to a 'primacy of honour' there must be added a 'primacy of responsibility'.

Without endeavouring for the moment to bring such language into line with the theological terminology of Roman Catholic doctrine, surely it is not impossible to hope that, by going deeper into these ideas and by bringing out what is contained in them, a notable approach may be made towards many points of the doctrine of the papacy as held by Roman Catholics. A line of study which is now being pursued in the Anglican Church seems to tend in that direction.[1]

Some divergence of view concerning the doctrine of the papacy was inevitable amongst those who took part in the Malines Conferences. But it is not of so radical a nature as to prevent the question being taken up again on a future occasion, and discussed afresh, with a great prospect of further advance in agreement of heart and spirit.

The importance of such conclusions reached by Christians apparently so far separated, needs no emphasis. And Lord Halifax's speech at the Albert Hall on 9 July 1925 (*supra*, p. 152) was important, even though it expressed only his personal opinions.

The Report seems hardly to notice M. Portal, though he was the very soul of the conversations. It was he who, together with his friend Lord Halifax, first conceived the idea of consulting Cardinal Mercier on the difficult problem of the reunion of the Churches. Although confident of the ultimate success of his work, he was not fully convinced of the possibility of uniting, *hic et nunc*, two ecclesiastical bodies which had for so many centuries developed along different lines. He was more concerned to encourage among churchmen a frank interchange of views, which he thought would

[1] See two articles in Theology (August and October 1926) by Dr. Turner on 'St. Peter and St. Paul in the New Testament and in the early church'.

lead to both sides getting a clearer and more accurate knowledge of the other's standpoint.

At the Malines Conversations M. Portal spoke very little ;
nor did he contribute any written Memorandum, but he was
at pains to stress the Anglicans' friendly attitude, and especially the Christian humility of their Bishops in their offer to
accept reordination. Although he never interfered with
the Cardinal's conduct of the meetings, he seemed to infuse
him with his ideas and his firm dislike of all mere controversy.
So the Cardinal, who had at first probably looked for individual conversions, came to accept the possibility of corporate conversions. He recognized in the Anglicans, at Malines,
deeply held religious convictions which were not incompatible with wide temperamental and intellectual divergences.

The fundamental difference between M. Portal and his
co-religionists, both in England and on the continent, was
that he sought merely to enlighten his questioners on their
respective positions, whereas they were more concerned
with immediate individual conversions. Most Catholic
journalists were caught with the idea that the only possible
good that could come out of the Malines Conversations was
the immediate reunion of the Churches. To M. Portal it
was enough that there had emerged a clear statement of
differing theological opinions, the resolution of which, together with the final reunion, he was content to leave to
the future.

CHAPTER 10

The Apostle of Love — Javel — Death of M. Portal

ANYONE reading only those chapters which describe M. Portal's public work for reunion, would fail to get a true or complete picture of the man. To know a man one must see him both in his public life and in the intimacies of his home life, which, in M. Portal's case, means among the poor and those Christian women whom he trained and directed in their work for the poor.

It is true that it was not difficult to see that this great apostle of union, entirely in his element among theologians and intellectuals, was nevertheless essentially a father and friend to all whom he helped or counselled: with him learning and friendship could never be divorced, since God had given to man both an intellect and a heart. But to understand better his humility, his simplicity, his active kindness, to realize how fully he lived as the faithful disciple of St. Vincent of Paul, one must see him in his more modest and less known work, but one perhaps dearer to his heart — simply a work of love.

The mission of Jesus Christ [M. Portal once said] is to preach the Gospel to the poor, but it is the particular mission of the disciples of St. Vincent, and I would be more than grateful if the Master would one day want me for that work.

To relieve misfortune was for M. Portal as much a natural necessity as a virtue. He had long meditated on the life of his beloved Master, and used to remark that our Lord's commission to His apostles to preach the Gospel always included healing the sick and feeding the hungry.

He refused to separate what his Master had made one : *facere et docere*. The following passage from advice he later gave to some charitably minded women, whom he directed, reads as an outpouring of his soul :

> For love our Lord became man ; nay more a poor man. He became one of the working class, the people. He did not only do good to the people, He incorporated Himself into them. You must do the same ; become the people, share their sorrows, enter into their interests, serve them.
> Our Lord atoned for our sins and redeemed us. If we really love the poor and the children, we will take on ourselves their sins and do penance on their behalf. The good shepherd gives his life for the sheep. Our Lord accepted humiliation. The cradle at Bethlehem, the Cross on Calvary, and the Eucharist are all acts of infinite self abasement, so that He may come to us, and feed our souls with His divine life. That is the path you must follow to reach the poor man's soul. If you believe our Lord's teaching, you will see in the poor the representatives of Jesus Himself. With what respect and humility should you approach them.

It is not surprising that someone like the young Fernand Portal should have been attracted to St. Vincent of Paul, and become a Lazarist with the firm intention of imitating our Lord under the guidance of that great friend of the poor and apostle of love. Throughout his life the Saint's life and writings were a great inspiration to him, and one day he too got together a band of ladies and asked them to devote themselves to works of corporal charity.

JAVEL

Like St. Vincent, whenever M. Portal was convinced that some favourite project was in accordance with God's will, he kept keen watch for some providential event to confirm his belief. In the case of reunion, a clear instance of such divine guidance was his unexpected meeting with

Lord Halifax in a foreign country to which he had gone for his health. As regards the work now to be described it came in an equally unexpected visit which a lady of the world paid to this humble Lazarist priest.

On 19 April 1907 this lady[1] called at No. 88 rue du Cherche-Midi, and told M. Portal of her recent great bereavement, and how, in her sorrow, she had made a pilgrimage to the Church of the Sacré-Cœur, Montmartre, and there resolved to seek consolation in devoting her life to acts of penitence and works of charity. She had fixed on the poor district of Javel, where hardly priest or sister of mercy could penetrate, and there, in no religious garb and without any propaganda, had striven to bring help and succour to the poor wretches who lived there. One must have known Javel as it was in 1906 to appreciate the marvellous daring of such an enterprise. It was a wretched and dangerous district where the inhabitants lived in abject poverty in the most dreadful hovels. The police were rarely to be seen in the dark and dangerous streets, which at night often reverberated with revolver shots. The wretched children who swarmed on the pavements and yards, played in the gutter with old rags and garbage: many had never set foot in a school or church, or heard God's name spoken.

A cobbler's house with a small garden, next door to a shop, had been rented and opened as the first day nursery. Soon, however, it was full and children had to be turned away. What was to be done? It was unthinkable to turn one's back on all this misery crying out for help. Surely some way must be found for enlarging one's premises, and one's compassion. And so this improvised sister of mercy, somewhat hesitatingly, called on M. Portal to seek his advice and help. At once he saw in this the answer to his hopes and prayers. He blessed and encouraged the work, and soon afterwards himself went to see the day nursery in the

[1] It was a Madame Gallice, widow of a M. Octave Gallice. See *L'Amitié au service de l'union*', by the Abbé Gratieux, p. 157.—A. T. M.

rue Alphonse, where he was greatly moved by the work going on there. The work must certainly be extended, he said: one cannot deny such service to God and God's needy children. On 6 January 1908 much larger premises, capable of taking a hundred and thirty children instead of thirty, were rented. Within twenty-four hours it was full to overflowing, and clearly too small. All the better, one would take a still larger house as soon as possible.

In the meantime, some organization was necessary. M. Portal preached a modest mission in Paris, and succeeded in getting together a number of generous and capable women. A school of domestic science was started, where singing and literature were taught, as well as cooking and dressmaking, also first aid. The original helpers formed a Union, and later a club for the younger women was started, which met on Sundays and Thursdays. In addition, holiday camps for little girls and younger women were organized, and they were taken to enjoy a healthy holiday in Normandy, Saint-Germain, and later to the Savoy.

M. Portal was radiant with joy, being at last in his element among the poor and needy whom he loved as a father. He delighted in talking to the children, to many of whom he brought their first knowledge of God.

Meanwhile in Javel itself, the work met with jealousy and persecution which, so far from discouraging M. Portal, seemed to him a mark of divine approbation.

But the few ladies who were helping were not enough. They lived a long way off, and so had far to come; and difficulties began to increase. What was needed was some women who would live in, on the spot where the work was being done. Remembering how St. Vincent had started his Daughters of Charity, M. Portal dreamed of starting something similar, a small core of women, not bound by any religious vows, but by the great ideal of divine love; living together and working for the four hundred and fifty children whom it was planned to accommodate at night as well as by day. This needed a much larger house, and a

site in the rue de Lourmel was bought.[1] Plans were made
and the building started. But, alas, every advance seemed to
bring its own troubles. The foundress, who devoted herself
and her fortune to the work, and on whom M. Portal relied
greatly, became seriously ill, and was advised by her doctors
that unless she left Javel, she would not live more than three
months. In the midst of the resulting anxiety and indecision
the true son of St. Vincent emerges. He said that 'If we
had known of this illness a fortnight back, I think we would
not have begun the work. But seeing that we did decide
and that the work has begun, to stop now would show lack
of faith.' And so, thanks to M. Portal's invincible faith, the
work was completed.

In 1914 war broke out, causing more anxiety. Again
M. Portal encouraged all, and translating words into deeds,
decided to adapt part of the house for use as a hostel for
refugees. Later the decision was taken to start a home for
war orphans. At once M. Portal left Paris to look for a
house in the country. His instinct took him to the Savoy,
and there he found the estate of 'Corbières', in a beautiful,
quiet situation on the slopes of Mont Revard above the lake
of Bourget, and only a few kilometres from Aix-les-Bains.
It was bought, and on 17 February 1917 the first batch of
orphans arrived.

It was one of M. Portal's great joys to go there to rest
from the tiring life of Paris, and he felt great elevation of
spirit in the contemplation of the mountains and far horizons.
There, among his own children, he was completely at ease,
and for them, too, his arrival was a red letter day. He mixed
perfectly with them, played with them, told them stories,
and generally spoilt them. And in the chapel he would
give them simple instruction in things pertaining to God.

But M. Portal did not want the work to become sta-
tionary. Between 1905 and 1925 there had been great
changes in the district of Javel. It had ceased to be a

[1] The conveyance was dated 16 February 1909 : see Gratieux, *op. cit.* p.
159.—A. T. M.

working-class district and become a business one, easily accessible to both clergy and sisters of mercy. So in order to remain true to the vocation of seeking always the down and out, a slummy district in the suburbs was sought. The table land of Kremlin-Bicêtre was chosen, and the building of a children's dispensary begun. It was opened on Friday, 18 June 1926, the day before M. Portal died, and gave him one of his last joys in this life, although not completely fulfilled, as he hoped that ultimately the Ladies of Javel would be sufficient in number for some to be able to go to live among the workers in this district.

DEATH OF M. PORTAL

In 1907 M. Portal wrote, 'I would like to die in Javel, in the midst of the poor, and the works of love'. And he added, 'May God grant us both an understanding of the poor and of the needs of the Church and strength to serve them to the end; and finally to die in full harness'.

Nearly twenty years later his prayer was granted. Although full of anxieties about the Malines Conversations and the prospects for the future, it was to the house in the rue de Lourmel that he had himself taken on 17 June when the first warnings of his last illness came upon him. There he was nursed by the Ladies of Javel, who watched by him, and at the last, sadly and reverently, closed his eyes, while downstairs the children prayed for their dying Father. On 19 June 1926 Fernand Portal departed from this world, and his soul at last enjoyed the vision of that divine union which he had so long loved. A year later his body was taken to Corbières and placed in the crypt of the chapel of Christ the Redeemer, where it awaits the resurrection of the dead.

M. Portal did so love the mountain with its exhilarating air. 'Our dear mountain', he used to say, 'is unequalled for raising one's thoughts Godwards. The old monks were quite right to seek to be near nature.'

Here he must often have reflected on his approaching

end. He had, at different times, expressed a wish that, when he was dead, his body might rest near a chapel to which people would come to pray for the reunion of all Christians.

I asked our Lord [he wrote in October 1919] to accept our sacrifice, and to allow us to work that men might come to love Him. I besought Him to bless our projects, and that from our mountain sanctuary there might flow a stream of love of God and suffering man . . . a small stream truly, but our small streams which flow into the Lake are so lovely and so precious. [Again in 1921] How I would like, before departing this life, to see our Chapel finished and opened for prayer. . . . A centre of prayer alongside a centre of works of charity, this is indeed the Christian ideal.

And now this hope, this prayer are fulfilled. On the slopes of Mont Revard, dominating the beautiful lake which Lamartine loved so much, and amidst the green of trees and fields, rises the white cupola of a Roman Byzantine chapel. It is dedicated to Christ the Redeemer. The theme of the entrance porch, copied from Chartres, shows Jesus surrounded by the emblems of the Evangelists, and at once elevates the thought to the one and only Saviour. In the choir is a large stained-glass window which shows our Lord surrounded by the Eleven, coming out of the upper room into a countryside of vines and corn, and making His great prayer, 'that they may be one even as We are one'. On the left an Epiphany shows all the gentile races acknowledging the kingship of Jesus Christ; while on the right is seen the blessed Virgin rising in glory from her tomb, encouraging us to trust that the Mother of us all joins her prayers for the reunion of her separated children.

There, in the crypt of that chapel for which he himself chose the site, and the shimmering whiteness of which attracts the traveller from afar, rest the mortal remains of Fernand Portal, servant of Christ and apostle of unity. Thither men will come, not to admire the mountains and scenery, but to spend a few moments in prayer and recollection near the body of him, the contemplation of whose great soul raises one's own soul higher than any mountain.

Thither will come as well, the friends he has left, and the future generations whom he could not know. They will come, as he often said, to seek the assurance of success in the remembrance of his sorrows and sacrifices.

From all the mountains surrounding the Lac de Bourget, from north, south, east, and west, descend both large and small streams, combining to form one sheet of water reflecting the blue sky above. And the day will dawn when from every part of the Christian world will come great souls who, like those others present though invisible, will continue to hope and to pray. And these will, in their union, form the Great Church, One, in which men will discern, more clearly, God's divine image revealed in Jesus Christ.

'Well done, good and faithful servant : enter thou into the joy of thy Lord.'

APPENDIX

Text of Letter, dated 15 *October* 1894,
from the Archbishop of Canterbury (*Dr. Benson*)
to Lord Halifax : see page 50

Addington Park
Oct. 15th, 1894

My dear Lord Halifax,

I need scarcely say how much thought I have given to your late visit to me at Baron's Down. I need not assure you that I can conceive of no greater privilege or happiness than to be used by our Lord as an instrument in realising that unity which He treats as the consummation of His Gospel. I am sure that you hold that there could be no unity except on the basis of Truth, and that you would be the first to impress on me that this responsible position of mine binds me above all not to risk Truth for the sake of any policy of unity.

If I had known, when you asked for that interview, that M. Portal would accompany you, I would have pointed out that my position almost required that I should be informed beforehand of any very grave matter which he had to lay before me, and I will ask you now kindly to excuse anything that could possibly seem harsh, by remembering that my interview with him was a great surprise. The sum of what then passed was this :—

M. Portal gave me a copy of a letter from Cardinal Rampolla to himself based on the representations which M. Portal had made to his Eminence of the state of Religion in England. The letter breathes a spirit of charity and strong desire for unity, but is written in very general terms which do not commit its author to any definite statement, but he apparently regards with satisfaction the arguments with which M. Dalbus (and M. Duchesne) combat the unfounded difficulties raised by ordinary Roman Catholics as to the validity of English Orders. M. Portal added that he knew from the very highest authority that M. Duchesne (whose views are known) is to be entrusted with the production of full researches upon the question. He (M. Portal) had himself had personal experience of the amicable views of this authority.

It is important to observe that M. Portal desired that this communication should be *private*, but he wished me to express in writing a favourable reception of it.

I must first say, as I said then, that the Archbishop of Canterbury is not in a position to take a private and unofficial line with secret agents from great powers. It is not our English method of procedure. It is not possible for me to say more upon that letter than that I also most deeply desire and pray that all the dissensions of Christendom might be ended, and rejoice that others long for it.

But among its kindly lines that letter contains expressions totally inadmissible and inconsistent with the primitive model to which England appeals.

But what is most important is that at this very time (before and since that interview) the head and representative of the Roman Catholic Church in England is officially declaring in a series of public utterances the absolute and uncompromising repudiation by the Papal See of the Orders of the Anglican Church.

How is it possible to weigh the private conversation of a private person on the private sentiments of a great power against the open declarations of the one most dignified and accredited agent of the same power? Whatever you may believe as to those private views you cannot wish me to ignore the fact that Cardinal Vaughan has spoken with an authority that nothing but public authority can contradict.

I shall await with the utmost interest the result of M. Duchesne's research, and also its reception by the Pope.

It is impossible that any step could be taken whilst the validity of our English Orders remained unacknowledged. And I shall then venture to hope that further investigations may be deemed not impossible on the part of the Roman Catholic Church into that doctrine and practice of the primitive Church to which the English Church appeals.

Meantime the spirit of Love which Cardinal Rampolla also invokes is the best preparation for fruitful investigation. 'Pectus facit Theologum', and no one will rejoice more than I if Theology working in that spirit leads Christians to perfect Unity in the Truth.

A. C. Benson, *Life of Edward White Benson*, Vol. II, p. 604.

BIBLIOGRAPHY

GENERAL

Bivort de la Saudée, J. de. *Anglicans et Catholiques: le problème de l'union anglo-romaine, 1833–1933.* Paris (Plon), 1949.

— *Documents sur le problème de l'union anglo-romaine, 1921–1927.* Paris (Plon), 1949.

Gratieux, A. *Trois Serviteurs de l'unité chrétienne: le père Portal, Lord Halifax, le cardinal Mercier.* Paris (Ed. du Cerf), (1937).

— *L'Amitié au service de l'union.* Paris (Bonne Presse), 1950.

Lockhart, J. G. *Charles Lindley, Viscount Halifax.* London (Geoffrey Bles), 1935.

THE ANGLO-ROMAN CAMPAIGN (Chapter 3)

Bell, G. K. S. *Randall Davidson,* vol. i, pp. 228 ff. Oxford (O.U.P.), 1935.

Benson, A. C. *Life of Edward White Benson,* vol. ii, ch. 11. London (Macmillan), 1900.

Halifax, Lord. *Leo XIII and Anglican Orders.* London (Longmans, Green), 1912.

Lacey, T. A. *A Roman Diary and other Documents connected with the papal Inquiry into Anglican Orders.* London (Longmans, Green), 1910.

Leslie, A. *Cardinal Gasquet,* ch. v. London (Burns, Oates), 1953.

Snead-Cox, J. G. *Life of Cardinal Vaughan,* vol. ii, ch. v. London (Burns, Oates), 1910.

THE MALINES CONVERSATIONS (Chapter 9)

Bell, G. K. A. *Op. cit.* vol. ii, ch. lxxix.

Bolton, A. *A Catholic Memorial to Lord Halifax and Cardinal Mercier.* London (Williams & Norgate), 1935.

The Conversations at Malines: Official Report of the Anglican Participants. Oxford (O.U.P.), 1927.

Frere, W. H. *Recollections of Malines.* London (Centenary Press), 1935.

181

Bibliography

Halifax, Lord. *The Conversations at Malines: Original Documents.* London (Philip Allen), 1930.

Mercier, Cardinal. *L'Unité chrétienne: textes et discours.* Amay s/Meuse (Irenikon-Collection, 3-4), 1927.

Oldmeadow, E. *The Life of Cardinal Bourne.*

Prestige, G. L. *The Life of Charles Gore,* pp. 478-489. London (Heinemann), 1935.

PRINTED BY R. & R. CLARK, LTD., EDINBURGH